JOHN WITTICH

Discovering London's Inns and Tavens

Highgate Literary & Scientific
Institution

SHIRE PUBLICATIONS LTD

Contents

British Library Cataloguing in Publication Data: Wittich, John. Discovering London's inns and taverns. — 3rd ed. I. Title. 647.95421. ISBN 0-7478-0166-5.

ACKNOWLEDGEMENTS
All photographs are acknowledged to Cadbury Lamb. The maps are by Robert Dizon. The cover is from a print of an inn yard by Cecil Aldin.

Printed in Great Britain by C. I. Thomas & Sons (Haverfordwest) Ltd, Press Buildings, Merlins Bridge, Haverfordwest, Dyfed SA61 1XF.

Introduction

Towards the end of the twelfth century, William Fitzstephen, secretary to the saintly Thomas Becket, Archbishop of Canterbury, wrote of London in his biography of his master. Beginning the Prologue with an elaborate dedication to Becket, Fitzstephen then comments on London and its inhabitants: 'The only plagues of London are the immoderate drinking of fools and the frequency of fires.'

The public house, a place set aside for the sole purpose of supplying drink to the passer-by, has in many ways taken the place of two distinct types of establishment — the inn and the tavern. There was always a difference between the two in law. At an inn one could obtain lodgings and meals as well as drinking the local brew of ale, whereas a tavern was a house where it was strictly forbidden to serve anything except drinks. The records show a number of innholders and tavern-keepers being fined for failing to observe the law in this matter.

The first inns, in a form we would recognise today, were a development of the Saxon alehouse; they evolved through the medieval church-hostels into the inns or hotels of the present day. The word 'inn' is of Saxon origin; at first it meant a chamber or bedroom, but later it came to mean a suite of rooms in which one lived. An excellent example of this use is the Inns of Court, where chambers (suites) are set aside as living quarters for lawyers.

A German ambassador who stayed in an English inn in 1129 recorded his appreciation in what must be the first visitors' book. He wrote: 'The inns of England are the best in Europe, and the Fountain, wherein I am now lodged as handsomely as I were in the king's palace, the best in Canterbury.'

The medieval inn served travellers only and provided merely the bare necessities. A guest would find an earthen floor, sometimes paved with stone slabs, and occasionally covered with rushes, although this was a luxury provided only in places where rushes were easily available; such inns that London possessed at that time would certainly not have had them. The guests slept in dormitories, shared by both sexes. The traveller would have a pallet on his share of the floor and would probably supply his own food or have some brought in from a nearby public cookhouse. The charge for the service was low. Records of journeys made by fellows of Oxford and Cambridge colleges still survive in some of the college archives. The Warden and two fellows of Merton College, Oxford, were charged one halfpenny for their beds, a farthing for candles and a farthing for soup. There were complaints about overcharging even in those days, and laws were passed to protect the traveller from being cheated.

Not only the brewers but also the Church brewed and sold ale.

The ingredients were provided by the parishioners, and the church ale was sold in aid of the church funds. In the records of St Peter's church, West Cheap, burnt down and not rebuilt after the Great Fire of 1666, an entry for 1447 shows that eighteen shillings and four pence was raised in this way.

Hops were first cultivated in England in 1070 but not used in beer making until 1390. An official eye was always kept on the price and quality of the beer made and sold in the City of London. In the fifteenth century Richard Whittington, four times Mayor of London, prosecuted the Brewers' Company for allowing the selling of dear ale — and won the case with costs.

In 1589 there were a thousand taverns in the City of London, and Lord Chancellor Bacon suggested that a few might be closed. Successive Lord Mayors had tried to limit the drinking but had had no effect.

The seventeenth-century diarist Samuel Pepys recorded his impressions of the inns of London and elsewhere, and Charles Dickens in the nineteenth century described the gin palaces of the day. He stated that there was one tavern to every sixty houses on average and that the gin palaces had thousands of customers daily.

During the twentieth century regulations were introduced restricting the hours during which alcohol could be sold, but in 1988 the licensing laws were changed to enable drinking establishments to open all day — if they wished. The choice of opening hours was left to the individual breweries or their tenants.

There was a time when two kinds of building — churches and public drinking houses — were considered untouchable, but not so today: nowadays they may be altered or disappear altogether. In preparing this third edition of *Discovering London's Inns and Taverns* the author found that it was not unknown for an inn or tavern to be there one day and not long after to have gone, even though the brewers normally own the freehold of the land. Such is the march of progress in the late twentieth century.

The characters who have managed the drinking houses of London can still be found there today. Their dress may belong to the twentieth century but their hospitality and the welcoming atmosphere they create remain unchanged.

1
Nelson and his ports of call

Standing high on his column, Horatio, Lord Nelson, looks down on the inns and taverns at his feet with perhaps a little regret that his present situation no longer allows him to sample the wares of the places he knew so well.

Because of its close proximity to the former Admiralty House, Whitehall makes an appropriate start to the taverns of this area. The **Silver Cross** (1) is on the site of the Hermitage of St Katharine, which was first mentioned in 1253. Edward III gave an annual allowance of thirteen shillings and four pence to the hermit here. The house was first licensed as a tavern in 1674 at a time when the property was owned by Joseph Craig, a member of the Board of Green Cloth. Taking its name from the Green Cloth that covers the table at which its business is transacted, the Board of Green Cloth is an ancient institution of the Royal Household. Its jurisdiction covers the licensing of taverns within the verge of the Court. It meets once a year in February and consists of the Master of the Household and five others. To this day the landlord of the Silver Cross has to renew his licence annually with the Board of Green Cloth at Buckingham Palace, a custom that dates from the time when the tavern stood on the verge of St James's Palace grounds. The present building is long and narrow and its interior is distinguished by a barrel-vaulted roof. Over the fireplace is a portrait of a Tudor maiden whose ghost is said to haunt the upper floors.

Turning left on leaving the Silver Cross, the walker soon reaches the **Clarence** (2), an eighteenth-century house whose signboard shows a clarence, a type of carriage, after which the house is named — 'a closed four-wheeled carriage, carrying four persons inside and two out'. It was named after the Duke of Clarence, later William IV. Sawdust on the floor, gaslights on the walls and relics of yesterday are all added attractions. A colourfully attired minstrel sometimes entertains on several nights during the week. It stands on the corner of Great Scotland Yard, once a palace where the Scottish kings stayed when visiting London.

At the other end of Great Scotland Yard is Northumberland Avenue and across the way is the **Sherlock Holmes** (3). Of all the great characters of fiction Holmes and Doctor Watson must be amongst the most popular; interest in them is as keen today as it has ever been. It is said that Holmes was created by Sir Arthur Conan Doyle while waiting for his patients to attend his surgery. Walks around London in search of places associated with Holmes are very popular. Here the walls of the bars are decorated with Holmes memorabilia and objects connected with his cases. Upstairs, on the way to the restaurant, is a reconstruction of the front room at number 221B Baker Street, complete with the bust supplied by Madame Tussauds when it was learnt that a sniper had been hired to shoot Holmes from the upstairs window of a nearby house. A correspondent in the American press commented a few years ago that 'until the world's press print an official obituary to Sherlock Holmes he lives on', a sentiment with which all members of the Sherlock Holmes Society will agree.

On leaving the Sherlock Holmes, turn right and walk up Northumberland Street to the Strand. Cross over the road and walk up the pedestrian area at the east end of St Martin in the Fields church to Chandos Place. Here is the **Marquis of Granby** (4), shown on earlier maps as the Hole-in-the-Wall. Here Claude Duval, the famous highwayman, was taken captive while drunk; this was just as well, for he was armed with three pistols at the time. Under its old name the house had been kept by Mother Maberley, a mistress of the licentious George, Duke of Buckingham. After the battle of Warburg during the Seven Years War in the eighteenth century the Marquis of Granby ordered 300,000 pints of porter to be drunk in honour of the occasion. Owing to his generosity to retired members of his regiment when they left the army, many of them opened public houses, and today innumerable inns bear the name of their benefactor — the Marquis of Granby.

In times past the **Salisbury** (5) in St Martin's Lane, once called the Coach and Horses and later Ben Caunt's Head, after the landlord better known as the Nottinghamshire Giant, was well known

The Tom Cribb, Panton Street.

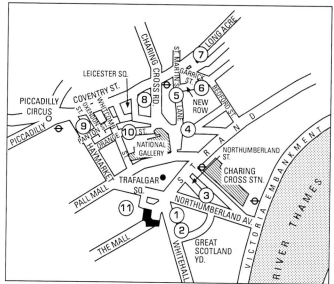

WALK 1: NELSON AND HIS PORTS OF CALL
1. The Silver Cross
2. The Clarence
3. The Sherlock Holmes
4. The Marquis of Granby
5. The Salisbury
6. The White Swan
7. The Lamb and Flag
8. The Bear and Staff
9. The Tom Cribb
10. The Hand and Racquet
11. The Two Chairmen

for the prize fights organised within its bars. Early in the nineteenth century Jim Belcher's comeback from early retirement was arranged here against the Game Chicken; history does not record the result. The sign depicts the third Marquis of Salisbury, from whom the site was leased in 1892. (It then traded as the Salisbury Stores.) In 1963 a major restoration brought it back to its original late Victorian splendour, now much appreciated by regulars from the surrounding theatres.

A short step from the Salisbury to New Row brings the traveller to the **White Swan** (6), a famed tavern since 1789. It has a reputation for helping ladies in distress. Charles Dickens used the tavern in several of his books. The *Epicure's Almanack* for 1815 recorded that the White Swan was a long-established house, well-known for the excellence of its fish, flesh and fowl, which were served in the best style of cookery daily to numerous respectable guests.

Tucked away off the beaten track is the **Lamb and Flag** (7), whose address is actually 33 Rose Street. For four hundred years it has been the haunt of theatregoers and theatricals. Its sign, identical to that of the Middle Temple Inn of Court, may have been of religious origin, although exactly why here is a mystery. Like its near neighbour the Salisbury, the Lamb and Flag has been closely associated in the past with prizefighters. Indeed at one time its nickname was the 'Bucket of Blood'. This is another tavern that Dickens used and knew well from his associations with the area. One of the earliest street signs was seen here, with 'This is Rose Street 1623' carved upon it, and not far from the house John Dryden, the poet and playwright, was attacked by three ruffians as a result of some words he had written about one of Charles II's mistresses.

On the corner of Charing Cross Road and Bear Street, opposite Wyndhams Theatre, is the **Bear and Staff** (8). The building dates from 1878, when it was rebuilt. It is an interesting late nineteenth-century drinking house with its sign showing a bear chained to a post and being tormented by two dogs.

In Leicester Square nearby, the pedestrian soon finds himself in the part of the square carefully allotted to him by the Westminster City Council because most of the square is cut off from traffic. So the wanderer comes to Panton Street. A few yards along, on the corner towards the Haymarket, is the **Tom Cribb** (9). In Conan Doyle's *Rodney Stone* the Tom Cribb in Panton Street is known as Tom Cribb's Saloon because Tom Cribb was the landlord. He was a noted fisticuffs fighter in the eighteenth century and his picture is painted on the signboard on the front of the house. There are many prints of prizefighters on the walls inside.

Retracing your route to Whitcomb Street from the Tom Cribb, it is only a short distance to the **Hand and Racquet** (10), so called because the royal tennis court lay nearby. Royal or real tennis is the ancestor of all racket games. It is played in a large enclosed court, the oldest one to survive being at Hampton Court Palace.

By turning to the right down Orange Street and left at the Haymarket, the walker passes the Theatre Royal and Her Majesty's Theatre before reaching New Zealand House on the corner. After crossing the roadway by way of the road island and ignoring all temptations to take the short cut back to Trafalgar Square, Cockspur Street is reached. Here, tucked away from the main stream of traffic, is Warwick House Street. The house has long since disappeared, but the **Two Chairmen** (11), built about 1690, recalls a more leisurely way of travelling — by sedan chair. This small public house has an inn-sign which depicts two chairmen in seventeenth-century dress. The panel of the door of the chair bears the royal monogram of two interlocking Cs. From here it is only a short walk back to Whitehall.

The Hand and Racquet, Whitcomb Street.

9

2
Let's all go down the Strand

From the twelfth century the Strand has been the main road linking Westminster and the City of London and was once lined with the stately homes of bishops and nobles. In and around it today are a number of theatres, all of which are licensed for the use of their patrons. But there are also a number of other places of refreshment either in or near to the street.

Beginning at Charing Cross station, pause for a moment to admire the Victorian replica of the Eleanor Cross in the forecourt of the station, then turn right outside and walk away from Trafalgar Square.

Shortly after leaving the station turn right down Villiers Street until you come to John Adam Street This leads to the **St Martin's Tavern** (1). Its signboard depicts the story of St Martin of Tours sharing his cloak with the beggar and is a reminder that we are in the parish of St Martin in the Fields.

This area was once the riverbank and all the streets led down to the river, which has retreated some hundred yards with the building in the nineteenth century of the Embankment. In the eighteenth

The Coal Hole, Strand.

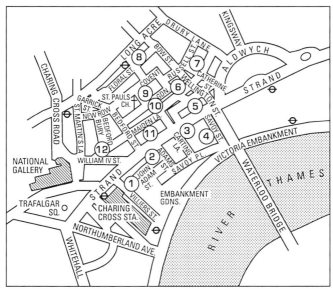

WALK 2: LET'S ALL GO DOWN THE STRAND
1. St Martin's Tavern
2. The George Adelphi
3. The Coal Hole
4. The Savoy Hotel
5. The Lyceum
6. The Gilbert and Sullivan
7. The Nell of Old Drury
8. The Nag's Head
9. The Punch and Judy
10. Rule's
11. The Peacock
12. The Lemon Tree

century the Adam brothers reclaimed the riverbank and built a series of streets and houses, calling it the Adelphi, the Greek word for brothers. One of the lanes which leads back to the Strand is George Court, where the **George Adelphi** (2) now stands, reminding the explorer that this land was once owned by George Villiers, Duke of Buckingham. It is said that the Emperor Napoleon Bonaparte lodged in this court between 1791 and 1792.

Having regained the Strand after leaving the George, turn right once more, and walk along to the **Coal Hole** (3) at the head of Carting Lane. In the early nineteenth century this tavern was a popular rendezvous for the coal-heavers who worked the Thames and who, after a long and tiring day, relaxed here in the evenings. The Wolf Room is a reminder of the club founded here by the actor Edmund Kean for repressed husbands who were not allowed to sing in their baths.

Further along the Strand is a place of legendary reputation, the

11

The Lyceum, Strand.

Savoy Hotel (4). The Savoy was built in 1889 on the site of the former royal palace of the Savoy, deriving its name from Peter of Savoy, whose statue stands on the exterior of the hotel and who came to England in 1241. All that is left of the palace and later hospital is the Queen's Chapel Royal, built in the early sixteenth century. This is approached down Savoy Street, the next turning on the right.

Cross the road to the **Lyceum** (5), whose signboard depicts an actor in front of his make-up mirror. He is preparing to appear on the stage of the Lyceum Theatre round the corner in Wellington Street. For peace and quiet try the taproom downstairs; the gardener will feel at home on the ground floor in the conservatory, while the weary can rest in the lounge on the first floor overlooking the Strand.

In Wellington Street can be found the **Gilbert and Sullivan** (6). The inn-sign portrays W. S. Gilbert on one side and Sir Arthur Sullivan on the other. The interior of the pub is filled with memorabilia of their operettas. Opposite there is a blue plaque commemorating Charles Dickens.

Although some authorities disagree, Nell Gwynne, the orange-selling mistress of Charles II, may have been born in a house in a lane or alley off Drury Lane. It is appropriate therefore that the **Nell of Old Drury** (7) should be found here in Catherine Street. Nell herself is buried in the church of St Martin in the Fields, and her funeral service was conducted by Thomas Tenison, the rector of the parish, who later became Archbishop of Canterbury. She was often seen on the stage of the Drury Lane Theatre, which is also in Catherine Street.

On the corner of James Street and Floral Street, behind the Royal Opera House, Covent Garden, is the **Nag's Head** (8). It was orig-

The Nell of Old Drury, Catherine Street.

The Punch and Judy, Covent Garden.

inally built as a hotel, drawing its clientele mainly from the opera house. Its inn-sign depicts a circus horse. It was also patronised by the porters of the Covent Garden market until the market was moved to Vauxhall. It is, however, still popular with the singers and dancers from the theatre.

Walk through Covent Garden, passing the portico of the church of St Paul, designed by Inigo Jones in the seventeenth century. Notice the stone in the wall recording that the first Punch and Judy performance in England — Punch's Puppet Show — was given here, witnessed by Samuel Pepys in 1662. Within the former market buildings is the **Punch and Judy** (9), with a sign and pictures on the walls depicting the theme of the puppet show. A balcony, at first-floor level, overlooks the piazza and from it the performances of the street-theatre actors can be enjoyed.

Follow Southampton Street to Maiden Lane, which runs parallel to the Strand. Here is **Rule's** (10), founded in the late eighteenth century and an accepted place of call for people interested in the theatre. Its gallery of portraits is without rival in the world of the theatre and includes all the great actors from Sir Henry Irving to the present day. When he was Prince of Wales, Edward VII regularly entertained Lily Langtry at Rule's. A special private entrance was built so that the Prince did not have to pass through the public restaurant. The hostelry has been referred to in books by Evelyn Waugh, Graham Greene and John le Carré.

Also in Maiden Lane is the **Peacock** (11), a comfortable house frequented by actors and stagehands alike. Over the bar is an illuminated window showing a peacock in all his glory.

14

Continue along Maiden Lane and cross into Chandos Place to the junction with Bedfordbury. You are walking in the footsteps of the famous and the infamous, for Charles Dickens frequented the area in his youth (as a blue plaque high on the left states) and the notorious highwayman Claude Duval was finally caught in the vicinity. Perhaps they visited the **Lemon Tree** (12) in Bedfordbury, the right-hand turning at the end of Chandos Place. Lemons were first introduced into England in the fifteenth century, but this public drinking house does not date back that far in history. Its proximity to the old Covent Garden fruit and flower market may well account for its name. In the *Daily Advertiser* of 6th April 1742 the Lemon Tree in Bedfordbury is mentioned as the place to enquire about the letting of a chapel in Great Queen Street — a strange role for a drinking house! Like other pubs hereabouts, it has many signed photographs of theatre people. It has been suggested that the various public houses around the former fruit and vegetable market were allotted to market workers according to their wares, and that here at the Lemon Tree may have gathered the citrus-fruit sellers. The house is popular with the orchestras from the Coliseum Theatre, whose stage door is next to the pub. Stay clear at interval time because the musicians have booked their drinks before the performance started and have little time to linger.

From here it is a short walk back to Charing Cross station and other public transport services.

Rule's, Maiden Lane.

Ye Olde Cock Tavern, Fleet Street.

3
Drink in the street of ink

The eastern end of the Strand joins Fleet Street, the history of which goes back to Roman times. It was once called Fleet Bridge Street for it led to the bridge over the river Fleet and on up Ludgate Hill to St Paul's Cathedral and beyond.

Records show that 'The Street', as Fleet Street is affectionately known across the world, had in the sixteenth century a number of printers living and working there. At that time the output of books, tracts and other printed material was considerable. Not all the printing was religious, but Latin grammars and readers were included. Wynkyn de Worde moved his printing press here from Westminster and printed, for the first time, *A mery geste of Robyn Hode and his Meyne*. Over the ensuing years printing and publishing developed to the extent that, until the 1980s, many national newspapers were printed here. Now they have all moved away with the exception of a few registered offices, and Fleet Street awaits a new identity.

A statue of Dr Samuel Johnson, who lived off Fleet Street, shares an island in the roadway with the parish church of St Clement Danes. He stands with his famous dictionary in his hand, looking down Fleet Street towards his favourite inns and taverns. One of the plaques on the plinth of his statue depicts him with James Boswell, his companion and biographer.

An original oil painting of George III incorporated into the façade of the **George** (1) explains how this inn acquired its name. It was rebuilt in the late nineteenth century and the architect created so perfect a Gothic building that many tourists must have mistaken it for a genuine medieval pub! It is well worth studying the exterior. Notice particularly the care that has been taken in creating the right atmosphere by including delightful carvings in the timbers of the building.

The George, Fleet Street.

Leaving the George, turn left outside and walk along to Essex Street to the **Edgar Wallace** (2). This may still be known to many people as the Essex Head, taking the name from Robert Devereux, Earl of Essex, a former owner of the land and house here. In 1975, the year of the centenary of the birth of Edgar Wallace, the public house was renovated and renamed the Edgar Wallace. The illegitimate son of an actress in Greenwich, Wallace became a famous war journalist, author of some of the finest crime stories ever written and a playwright and cinema scriptwriter. He died in 1932 and his body was brought back from Hollywood, where he was writing screenplays, and buried in the tiny churchyard at Little Marlow in Buckinghamshire.

Leading out of Essex Street, to the side of the Edgar Wallace, is Devereux Court, on the inner corner of which stands the **Devereux Arms** (3). It was originally the Grecian Coffee House, patronised by Sir Richard Steele, who wrote his learned articles here. Today the clientele consists largely of men of the law, their students, and others who have discovered this charming oasis behind the hustle and bustle of the Strand and Fleet Street. It first appears under its former title in a list of coffee houses published early in the eighteenth century and acquired its present name about a hundred years later. High above the main entrance to the house is a bust of a later Earl of Essex with the inscription 'This is Devereux Court, 1676'.

Not open to the general public but nevertheless a building to take note of in the walk is the **Wig and Pen Club** (4). Built in the early seventeenth century, it is a good example of a house that existed in London before the Great Fire of 1666. Today it is one of the best eating and drinking clubs in London, whose members, in the main, are all connected with the law or writing. Chivalry and the rules of the club still demand that a lady shall not be left alone in any of the bars, and if necessary a male member of the staff will keep a lady company until her own escort returns. The club stands just outside the City of London, whose boundary is marked by a monument in the middle of the roadway here, on the former site of Temple Bar.

Walking down Fleet Street away from Temple Bar, you will find **Ye Olde Cock Tavern** (5). Originally on the opposite side of the roadway, it was rebuilt on its present site in 1887, when the street was widened. All that is left of the former house is the inn-sign said to have been carved by the seventeenth-century woodcarver Grinling Gibbons. Pepys, Thackeray and Dickens all knew the house and recorded their visits to it. Samuel Pepys mentions a particularly comely wench, a certain Mrs Knipp. Like those of other public houses in the City, the hours of opening are different from normal hours. Closing time here is usually nine o'clock in the evening, and the place is closed on Saturdays and Sundays.

A City Corporation blue plaque marks the site of Dr Johnson's favourite tavern, the Mitre in Fleet Street, but just behind, in Mitre Court, there is the **Clachan** (6), a building of the twentieth century

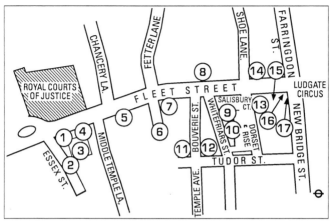

WALK 3: DRINK IN THE STREET OF INK

1. *The George*
2. *The Edgar Wallace*
3. *The Devereux Arms*
4. *The Wig and Pen Club*
5. *Ye Olde Cock Tavern*
6. *The Clachan*
7. *El Vino's*
8. *Ye Olde Cheshire Cheese*
9. *The Coach and Horses*
10. *The Harrow*
11. *The Witness Box*
12. *The White Swan*
13. *Ye Olde Cogers*
14. *The Poppinjay*
15. *The Old Bell*
16. *The Punch Tavern*
17. *The Albion*

but with ancient associations. If you are in the vicinity on the night before a rugby international, come here and sing your heart out, and quench your thirst as well. By day the Clachan is the haunt of barristers and law students.

El Vino's (7), once described as being frequented by judges, Queen's Counsel and journalists, is not strictly speaking a tavern or an inn but a place of good refreshment. Dylan Thomas, the Welsh poet, was a constant visitor during his time in London. The house is still a social centre for Fleet Street, and its distinctive Victorian atmosphere belies the fact that it was built only in the early decades of the twentieth century. This is because most of the furniture and fittings come from the company's property built in Mayfair in 1879 and removed here early in the twentieth century.

Perhaps the most famous of all the inns and taverns of Fleet Street is **Ye Olde Cheshire Cheese** (8) with its long connections with Dr Johnson and other literary figures. It was rebuilt shortly after the Great Fire of London in 1666, but the site is much older and covers the cellars of the house of the Abbots, later Bishops, of Peterborough. One of the most famous inhabitants of the inn was a parrot whose knowledge of abusive words was second to none. Its fame was widespread and people came from far and wide to listen to it speak. When it died, in 1926, at the alleged age of forty years, obituaries appeared in leading newspapers throughout the English-speaking world and also in the *North China Star*: 'Famed bird of blasphemy dies ... victim of pneumonia'. Even the BBC mentioned it in its newscasts. Dr Johnson's chair is still there, but there is little else to remind the visitor of the illustrious customers of the past.

Across the road from Wine Office Court is Whitefriars Street. Walk down the street until you reach the **Coach and Horses** (9), a nineteenth-century building whose sign depicts one of the early horse buses that were seen on the streets of London in Victorian times.

Further down the street is the **Harrow** (10) public house. The inscription by the door reads: 'The Harrow is over two hundred years old although a public house was known to have stood on this site longer.' The original Harrow consisted of just the larger downstairs bars. The back bar, which must be one of the smallest in the City, was once a tailor's shop where Oliver Goldsmith's tailor worked. As the newspaper industry grew, so did the number of people working in the area and the pub was extended into this adjoining shop. The story goes that the tailor's ghost may still be heard at work here. On the Primrose Hill side the pub has a Micawber Room and a Press Room. The sign on this side is of a model harrow.

Continue down Whitefriars Street to Tudor Street. The **Witness Box** (11) at the junction of Tudor Street and Temple Lane opens from 11 am to 11 pm Mondays to Fridays only. The ground floor is a restaurant with a bar in the basement. The sign shows a fur-coated lady in the witness box of a law court. A plaque on the outside of the building reads 'The British Institute of Innkeeping'.

The other way along Tudor Street is the **White Swan** (12), built by Adams Smith in 1881. The outside is decorated with terracotta swans and the arms of the Worshipful Company of Clothworkers of the City of London. Inside, the walls are covered with paintings and prints of London.

Continue along Tudor Street until Dorset Rise, and walk up the hill, passing on the left the blue plaque marking the site of the Salisbury Court Playhouse. Here is Salisbury Square, out of which leads Salisbury Court. A plaque marks the site of Pepys's birthplace, just before which is the Press Association, from whose building there projects a stone support for a lost inn-sign — that of **Ye Olde Cogers** (13), formerly called the Barley Mow. The building was designed by Sir Edwin Lutyens, architect of the Cenotaph in Whitehall. Its later title comes from the eighteenth-century debating society which used the house for its weekly meetings. They now meet in the Albion in New Bridge Street (number 17, below).

Opposite the Pepys plaque there is another that reads: 'The first number of the *Sunday Times* edited at 4 Salisbury Court by Henry White October 20th 1822.' The building was erected in 1878 with terracotta decoration showing the arms of the Worshipful Company of Vintners of the City of London.

Shortly afterwards Fleet Street is rejoined. Across the road from Salisbury Court is a new public house, opened in 1976, the **Poppinjay** (14). It is built on the site of 'the sign of the popyngaye' — the sign of the Abbots of Cirencester, whose house stood here in medieval times. Every May the Festival of the Poppinjay took place in the fields outside the city wall. A model bird was attached to a pole and used for target practice by archers. At the end of the day the winner was declared to be Captain Poppinjay. The stone in the entrance to the house weighs $2^{1}/_{2}$ tons and is made out of red Mansfield stone from Nottinghamshire. It formerly stood over an archway leading to Poppins Lane nearby.

Across the roadway is the **Old Bell** (15), with entrances both in Fleet Street and in the tiny lane that runs beside the nearby church of St Bride. During the rebuilding of the city after the Great Fire of

The Poppinjay, Fleet Street.

London priority was given to the quick reconstruction of many of the inns and the Old Bell was one of these. It still quietly serves the needs of its clientele, whether passers-by or members of the choir from the nearby church.

No visit to the pubs of Fleet Street is complete without a call at the **Punch Tavern** (16), particularly if you are a great admirer of the cartoons and articles that appeared in *Punch* magazine. It has a fine entrance elaborately decorated with Victorian tiles.

Just around the corner from Fleet Street in New Bridge Street is the **Albion** (17), a nineteenth-century pub with a twentieth-century sign showing John Bull, complete with a Union Jack waistcoat and standing on top of the White Cliffs of Dover. The Old Cogers Society now meets here every Saturday evening. Visitors are welcome but are not normally allowed to take part in the discussion. An ancient tradition was broken recently when a lady was elected as the President of the Society. Before this ladies were allowed to attend meetings but were enjoined to 'keep silent'.

You have now reached Ludgate Circus, with the memorial plaque to Edgar Wallace on the corner of Farringdon Street, and all the pubs of the City of London before you.

4
Jack London's abyss and
the Ripper's haunts

Arriving in London in about 1900, Jack London, the American novelist, made an intimate study of the area of the city 'just beyond Aldgate'. He used the information he obtained from his survey to form the basis of his novel *The People of the Abyss*, telling of the dreadful conditions under which the poor working-class people of London lived. Murders, rape and other violent crimes were commonplace, but none has captured the imagination of the public as much as the crimes committed by Jack the Ripper. Between August and November 1888 five prostitutes were murdered in the most brutal manner, and although several names have been suggested, including that of a member of the royal family, nobody was ever brought to trial for the crimes. The area is changing, Spitalfields market has been moved to Stratford East and its site has been prepared for development with offices and flats. Conservationists have moved in to protect the seventeenth-century houses and streets, and Christ Church, whose tall steeple dominates the area, is being restored to its former glory. The area where once Jack the Ripper stalked the streets by night is taking on a new look.

Purporting to be one of the oldest surviving licensed houses in London, the **Hoop and Grapes** (1) in Aldgate High Street was built in the seventeenth century, but originally served as a private house. The construction of the building is typical of the houses of the period and conveys something of the atmosphere of the city before the Great Fire destroyed five sixths of London in 1666. Notice the carvings on the posts at the entrance, the overhanging upper storeys, and, on entering the building, the narrowness of it. The bar and the kitchen are connected by an ear-shaped device in the wall, the forerunner of more sophisticated modern methods by which the barkeeper can communicate with the kitchen staff. Under the building there are sprawling cellars and passages, which are said to have linked the house with the Tower of London, or perhaps with the docks where smugglers and river pirates held sway. Over one of the window frames can be seen the parish boundary marks of the parishes of St Botolph's, Aldgate, and St Mary's, Whitechapel.

Hidden from the sight of the passer-by in Aldgate High Street, the **Still and Star** (2) is well worth searching out. It is in Little Somerset Street, a place linked with Jack the Ripper by those who think he may have been a butcher at one of the slaughterhouses in the neighbourhood. The origin of the name is obscure, although the Still may merely mean that an apparatus for the distillation of spirits was once

23

(Above) The Still and Star, Little Somerset Street.
(Below left) The Hoop and Grapes, Aldgate High Street.
(Below right) The Mail Coach, Camomile Street.

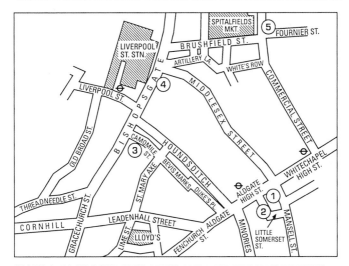

WALK 4: JACK LONDON'S ABYSS AND THE RIPPER'S HAUNTS

1. *The Hoop and Grapes*
2. *The Still and Star*
3. *The Mail Coach*
4. *Dirty Dick's*
5. *The Ten Bells*

kept here. It is certainly a rare name for a public house, although there is one in Sleaford, Lincolnshire, bearing the sign of the Still. The second half of the name may be explained as the sign of the Innholders' Company: the Star of Bethlehem that shone over the inn.

From here return to Aldgate across the new pedestrian area with its modern sculpture, and walk along Houndsditch to its junction with St Mary Axe on the left. Turn left and you will soon come to Camomile Street, where, in the basement of a modern office building, you can visit the **Mail Coach** (3). The signboard shows the mail coach being pulled by four sturdy horses with the driver and his assistant riding 'up-front' and a red-coated gentleman at the rear ready to blow his horn to warn tollgate and city gate keepers of their impending arrival. Behind the house, in Clerk's Place, is the blue plaque recording the site of the first hall of the Worshipful Company of Parish Clerks of the City of London.

From the Mail Coach turn left up to Bishopsgate and right along it. Leaving the former walled city of London by passing through the site of the old Bishopsgate, with the bishop's mitre on the wall just beyond Camomile and Wormwood Streets, but still remaining within the jurisdiction of the Lord Mayor, the walker reaches **Dirty**

Dirty Dick's, Bishopsgate.

Dick's (4), in Bishopsgate. According to the story, Nathaniel Bentley sealed up the room in which his wedding breakfast was to have taken place after his bride to be left him waiting at the church. He became a ragged eccentric. The room was later bought by the landlord of the tavern in Bishopsgate that today bears Bentley's nickname of Dirty Dick. Legend has it that Nathaniel had inherited the family hardware business from his father, attended the court of Louis XVI of France and became 'a most accomplished courtier' before he lost his bride. Although Bentley lived and died in Leadenhall Street, the landlord is supposed to have moved the room, lock, stock and barrel, to this site in Bishopsgate, the previous tavern being called the Gates of Jerusalem or the Old Port Wine House. It is well worthwhile descending to have a drink in this curious place.

From Bishopsgate take the second street on the right, Artillery Lane, and follow it until you reach the junction with Artillery Passage on the right. Here are recently restored eighteenth-century houses and shops. Across the roadway there is a multi-storey car park, the entrance to which is in White's Row. Walk down the Row to see, on your right, a fine seventeenth-century house with steps up to the door on the first floor. It has been restored to its former glory but is no longer used as a residence. White's Row leads into Commercial Street; turn left and shortly the parish church of Spitalfields, Christ Church, designed by Nicholas Hawksmoor in the eighteenth century, is seen on the corner of Fournier Street. Adjacent to it is the Ten Bells (5). Once called the Jack the Ripper, the walls were adorned with photographs of the places where the Ripper murdered his victims and with extracts from the *Illustrated Weekly Police* newspaper. It is generally accepted that there were five murders by the same person called Jack the Ripper; all five victims had their throats cut and were disembowelled. All were prostitutes and in their forties, except the last, Mary Kelly, who was also the only victim to have been murdered indoors; the rest were left on the streets.

The neighbourhood around the public house is interesting to explore but, for those wishing to return, Brushfield Street opposite the church will bring them shortly to Bishopsgate and Liverpool Street Station.

5
Along Old Father Thames's north bank

It has often been said that London's history is the story of its river, the Thames, and there are many old and interesting inns and taverns on its banks, some of which are especially attractive. This chapter describes those on the north bank. Those on the south bank are described in chapter 9.

Standing right on the edge of the Thames at Isleworth, the **London Apprentice** (1) commands a very good view of the river and has as its neighbour the parish church, whose tower dates from medieval times, though the rest of the building is modern because the previous church was burnt down by fire caused by young children playing with matches. A short distance away is the entrance gateway to Syon House, the London home of the Dukes of Northumberland, rebuilt in the eighteenth century to the designs of Robert Adam, the Scottish architect. Dominating one side of the inn is a painting of the London apprentice who, having spent the afternoon rowing on the river, stopped and refreshed himself at the inn. Rebuilt in the early eighteenth century, with a stucco ceiling in the upstairs lounge, today it is a scheduled building of great architectural interest and, although it no longer stays open all night as it did in earlier days, its popularity is as great as ever. The tavern is said to have been used as a secret meeting place by Henry VIII and Catherine Howard. Other royal visitors have included Elizabeth I and Charles II. History does not record whom they met here! Using the tunnel from the house to the nearby parish church, river smugglers would store their ill-gotten gains in the crypt of the church.

Standing back from the river and by the side of the Grand Union Canal (river Brent) is the **White Horse** (2) at number 24 Market Place, Brentford. Once the home of J. M. W. Turner, the artist, today it welcomes locals and visitors alike. It makes an excellent stopping place for those visiting Syon Park or the nearby Kew Bridge Steam Museum.

There are several attractive riverside inns and taverns at Chiswick's Strand on the Green, best approached by the road that leads off to the left as you face Kew Bridge from the north side. The first port of call is the **Steam Packet** (3), a reminder of the ships that plied for hire on the river in the nineteenth century. Travel by boat was then the cheapest and safest way; there was less chance of being robbed on the water than on the land.

At number 13 Thames Road, which runs parallel to the river, is the **Bell and Crown** (4), another favourite landing place for river pirates. Everything from watches to brandy was unloaded on the

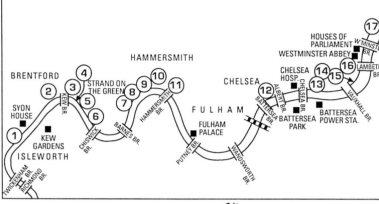

WALK 5: ALONG OLD FATHER THAMES'S NORTH BANK

riverside here. One recent landlord, Arthur Turpin, claimed descent from the most notorious highwayman of all times, Dick Turpin. A picture of a famous river smuggler's barge, the *Lady Edith*, hangs in the bar. From here it is a short walk back to the towpath along the riverside.

The next tavern stands by the towpath. It is the **City Barge** (5), and its sign clearly shows the reason for its name. The barges of the Lord Mayors of London were moored here in times when they, too, found the river to be the safest way of travelling. The river sometimes overflows its banks along this stretch so that the water laps against the walls of the inn. Consequently precautions have been taken to prevent flooding inside the building: there is a step before entering the bar, and at high tide beams are placed in a slot on the outside of the door frame. The licensees of the City Barge have charters which show that the original house on this site was built in Elizabethan times, but the site may be older still, for references to the City Barge at Chiswick occur in fifteenth-century documents. To have visited the inn five hundred years ago on a cold night would have been a pleasure; warm beer was served, heated by a red-hot

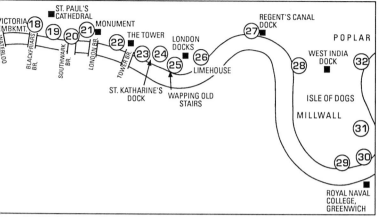

poker from the open fire placed into the tankard, and with a generous helping of ginger added. The bar is dominated by the seventeenth-century parliamentary clock with its open face. (If there had been a hinged glass door on the face a tax would have had to be paid to the government, so the face was left uncovered.)

Leave the City Barge, turn left outside the riverside bar and continue along the towpath. The railway bridge carrying Underground trains to Richmond is soon seen, and shortly beyond it is the **Bull's Head** (6). It was built in 1642 but looks like two eighteenth-century cottages knocked into one. It is rumoured to have been a secret hideout for Oliver Cromwell during the seventeenth century.

Downstream from Chiswick is the former village of Hammersmith, originating from a small hithe, or inlet in the riverbank, used for the loading and unloading of goods from boats. Accessible from the great West Road (A4) and from Hammersmith Terrace, the latter joining the Chiswick Mall and the Upper (Hammersmith) Mall, is South Black Lion Lane, the site for the past four hundred years of the **Black Lion** public house (7). It is famous for its skittle alley and for its prizewinning garden. The author A. P. Herbert, who lived nearby, renamed the house the 'Black Swan' in his book *The Water Gypsies*. Until 1963 the pub was the home of the Black Lion Skittle Club, who won fame, if not fortune, in the skittle alleys of London and the Home Counties.

At number 25 Upper Mall is the **Old Ship** (8), a late seventeenth-century riverside house that claims to be the oldest licensed tavern in Hammersmith. It is attractive both in the summer, when from the balcony one can watch the river and its activities, and in the winter, when open fires warm the outer body as the drink warms the inside. Around the walls are rudders, skiffs, lifebelts and other boating memorabilia.

At the end of Hammersmith Mall, a continuation of the Chiswick Mall, is a group of seventeenth- and eighteenth-century houses

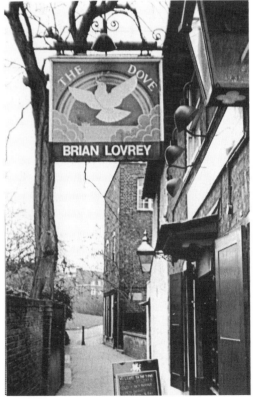

The Dove, Hammersmith.

served by the **Dove** (9) (strictly, it is in the Upper Mall). It was purchased by its present owners, Fuller, Smith and Turner, in 1796, although there was a riverside inn here in the seventeenth century, and Charles II and Nell Gwynne are said to have frequented it. William Morris lived in the house almost next door to the pub and so the Pre-Raphaelite artists were frequent visitors to the place, which appears in some of their paintings. In more recent years A. P. Herbert used the Dove, disguising it as the Pilgrim in his novel *The Water Gypsies*. 'Rule Britannia' is said to have been written in an upper room of the house. A plaque in the public bar shows the height of the high tide of 1928, and it is to be hoped that this mark will never be reached again. Brian Lovrey's inn-sign, over the main entrance of the building, shows the dove and the rainbow, although, through a mis-spelling in the nineteenth century, the pub has been known as the Doves. There is a grapevine near the verandah, a favourite place from which to watch the annual Oxford and Cambridge Boat Race.

Turn right outside the Dove and a short path leads to the riverside, Furnivall Gardens, Hammersmith Pier and the first close sight of Hammersmith Bridge. Along this stretch of the riverbank are several places of refreshment — rowing is a thirsty sport — including the **Rutland** (10), built originally in 1849, and the **Blue Anchor** (11), which was first licensed in 1720. Both attract visitors to their doors during the summer and conveniently provide seats for patrons who like to watch the river and its activities while drinking.

Chelsea has many attractions and one of its numerous places of refreshment is the **King's Head and Eight Bells** (12), on Cheyne Walk. The name arose from the fact that long ago it was the custom to ring the church bells when royalty was travelling on the river in the vicinity. Here, too, the overflow of people from the bars spreads out on to the pavement in the summer season.

A short distance from Chelsea Bridge along the Grosvenor Road is the **William IV** (13), the only public house between Vauxhall and Chelsea Bridges that is actually on the riverside. Built in early Victorian times, it is an excellent example of a Victorian drinking establishment. The clientele comes from two main sources, the nearby Churchill Gardens Estate, and Dolphin Square a short distance along the road. From the house there is a good view across the river to Battersea Power Station and the gasholders. A bust of the king stands proudly on the parapet at the front of the house.

Standing behind the William IV on the Churchill Gardens Estate and shielded from the noise of the traffic of Grosvenor Road is the **Balmoral Castle** (14). Built in 1856, it has been described as 'one of the most elegant examples of a London Victorian pub'. The style is classical Italian and, in spite of being left 'high and dry' when all the buildings around it were demolished in the 1950s to make way for the housing estate, it appears untouched by time and man alike. The interior is superbly decorated with mirrors and green, gold, red and black surrounds. This is the place to join the locals.

The **Morpeth Arms** (15) is situated by the Tate Gallery on land that once belonged to the notorious Millbank Penitentiary and has cellars that connect to a tunnel through which prisoners were escorted to barges that took them down river to the Upper Pool where they were transferred to larger sea-going ships for transportation to the colonies.

The **Marquis of Granby** (16) in Romney Street (just off Horseferry Road, which leads to Lambeth Bridge) is a listed building and is close enough to the local 'sights', Westminster Abbey and the Tate Gallery, but not on the usual tourist route. Its close proximity to the Houses of Parliament makes it a favourite haunt of members of both Houses. It is equipped with a division bell to summon them to Parliament when they are required to vote.

Moored by the Victoria Embankment between Westminster Bridge and Waterloo Bridge, the **PS Tattershall Castle** (17) offers drinkers a fine view across the Thames and the chance to partake of their favourite brew, whether it be tea or something stronger, in unique surroundings. The paddle steamer was built in West Hartlepool in 1938 by William Gray and Company and entered service with the North Eastern Railway as a ferry boat at Hull. When the Humber Bridge was opened in 1972 the boat became obsolete and was moved to its present site.

Soon the City of London is reached, with its numerous places of refreshment. Opposite Blackfriars station and on the corner of Queen Victoria Street is the **Black Friar** (18), whose present building dates from 1903, although its associations go back to 1278, when the nearby streets were given to the Dominican Order (the Black Friars). The first public house here was built in the seventeenth century, occupying a corner of the precinct of the priory. The decoration of the building is Art Nouveau; the work of Henry Poole RA, it is a rare combination of materials — marble, bronze, wood and glass — and depicts everyday life and events in the priory. On the outside wall is the figure of a Black Friar in his robes, while the signposts to the saloon bar are also worth noting.

The **Mermaid Theatre** (19) is the only permanent theatre within the City Wall and was the brainchild of the late Lord Miles of Blackfriars. Built originally in the shell of a burnt-out warehouse, it has since been developed and is now enclosed by an office building. It is a little-known fact that the River Room is technically a public bar attached to the theatre. The view from it across the river reveals the former Bankside Power Station, and the new Globe Theatre

The Morpeth Arms, Millbank.

Centre can also be admired. When the theatre is 'dark' (that is, when there is no performance) the opening hours of the bar are 4 pm to 9 pm, Mondays to Fridays.

Return to Upper Thames Street and continue towards the Tower of London. Shortly before London Bridge, on the corner of Arthur Street, is the **Porter's Lodge** (20). The sign shows the porter taking his rest here, a reminder of the close proximity of the Billingsgate Fish Market until its removal to West India Docks in 1981. Although the pub is built into a modern office building, the interior decoration resembles the library of a stately home, complete with wood-panelled alcoves, bookshelves, armchairs and settees.

The Olde Wine Shades, Martin Lane.

Amid modern office developments, in the quiet of Martin Lane, is El Vino's the **Olde Wine Shades** (21). It was built over three hundred years ago and miraculously survived the Great Fire of London of 1666 and the Blitz of 1940-1, although it is but a stone's throw from where the Fire started in a baker's shop in Pudding Lane. Here you may partake of your favourite sherry, port or other wine. Charles Dickens was a frequent visitor here and enjoyed its old-world atmosphere as much as present customers. Evidence of its pre-Fire origin is provided by the finely decorated lead cistern, which bears the date 1663. Early maps and writings refer to the house as the 'Sprague Shades', presumably after a former owner or licensee. A tunnel, now blocked, led down to the river and must surely be a relic of the smuggling that went on here. Opening hours are Mondays to Fridays only: 11.30 am to 3 pm, and 5 pm to 8 pm.

At the end of the longest street in the City of London, Thames Street (Upper and Lower), is the Tower of London, with the **Tiger Tavern** (22) opposite its main entrance. Founded in the sixteenth

century, though rebuilt in the twentieth century, this tavern has a long and interesting history. In the upper bar can be seen, by pressing a light switch on the wall, a mummified cat said to have been stroked by the young Princess Elizabeth (later Queen Elizabeth I) when she was imprisoned in the Tower. There are still remains of a tunnel that she used to reach the tavern under the moat and roadway, though both ends have now been securely blocked. Every ten years an interesting ceremony takes place here: the Lord Mayor of London, the sheriffs, aldermen and members of the Common Council come here, bringing with them their beer-tester to test the quality of the beer being sold. It is not by any modern scientific means that the test is made: some of the beer is poured on to a stool provided by the inspectors, and the tester then sits on it. If the man's breeches stick to the seat all is well — and it always is! When the ceremony is completed a garland is placed round the neck of the landlord and a bouquet of laurel leaves is hung outside the door.

Beyond the Tower of London, at St Katharine's Dock, a new development has arisen over the past few years centred round the

Tower Hotel (23), which has several restaurants and bars open to the general public. A new vista of the Thames has been opened up, from Tower Bridge downstream towards Greenwich. Many boats are moored in the marina, including several historic vessels such as the old *Nore* lightship and some sailing barges with their red sails.

Amongst the many eating places and shops in this area is the **Dickens Inn** (24), in a converted building previously part of a brewery in St Katharine's Dock. Opened in 1976 by the great grandson of Charles Dickens, the inn is a place of unusual interest. Its ground-floor bar serves only real ales, with not a single bottle in sight, while the upper floors provide food. On the top floor, in the Dickens Room, are held cabarets which have a special Dickensian theme.

When most of the trade of the London docks moved downstream to Tilbury many acres of land became available for redevelopment and Dockland is now being rebuilt as a commercial and residential area. Next to St Katharine's Dock was the London Dock but between the river and the dock Wapping High Street still runs. By going along St Katharine's Way and crossing the entrance to the London Dock the High Street is soon reached and just past the entrance to Wapping Basin is the **Town of Ramsgate** (25). Previously shown on maps as the Red Cow in deference to the colour of a former barmaid's hair, it was renamed the Town of Ramsgate after being adopted by the Ramsgate fishermen who used to sell their fish from Old Wapping Steps at the side of the public house. It was on these steps that 'Bloody' Judge Jeffreys was caught in 1688, disguised as a sailor, when trying to escape to Hamburg. He was recognised and taken to the Tower of London, where he died of a wasting disease. He was buried secretly in the church of St Mary Aldermanbury. When the church building was dismantled to be rebuilt in America the judge's grave was discovered, but the site has not been marked. Sailors found guilty of crime on the high seas were sentenced to death by being washed over by three tides at this point of the river. The water bloated the bodies, and the expression 'What a wapper' is said to have originally referred to somebody executed in the river here at Wapping. The tavern has a grisly history, with secret tunnels leading to the Tower of London and a garden that was once used as a hanging dock for petty thieves. Captain Kidd is said to haunt the pub.

Seen from the river or from the land the **Prospect of Whitby** (26) on Wapping Wall seems a small public house. Originally built in 1543, it is one of the oldest riverside public houses and was once known as the Devil's Tavern after its associations with the river thieves and smugglers. Samuel Pepys visited the place a number of times in the seventeenth century. Later in the same century Judge

The Waterman's Arms, Isle of Dogs.

Jeffreys came here to watch the river executions, and in the nineteenth century Charles Dickens is said to have used the Prospect as the Six Jolly Fellowship Porters in *Our Mutual Friend*. By Dickens's time the name had been changed from the Devil's Tavern to the Prospect of Whitby. The change came about because a ship called the *Prospect*, which was registered at Whitby in North Yorkshire, was moored off the tavern. The ship became a landmark and the tavern was referred to as the one by the *Prospect* of Whitby, and so this eventually became its name. In the early eighteenth century a sailor brought into the bar a flower that was then unknown to the local inhabitants. He sold the plant to a local market gardener, who used it to produce three hundred like it. The plant was the fuchsia and is still very popular with gardeners all over Britain. Here, too, came the artists J. A. McN. Whistler, J. M. W. Turner and David Cox to paint the beautiful sunsets over the river, and doubtless they sampled the brew of the tavern before they left.

From the Prospect of Whitby on Wapping Wall go back to The Highway and turn towards Stepney. When Narrow Street appears on the right-hand side walk down it and there you will find the **Grapes** public house (27). Like the Prospect of Whitby, it is situated beside the river, has an attractive verandah and claims to be the model for Charles Dickens's Six Jolly Fellowship Porters in *Our Mutual Friend*. The building dates from 1650, but the place is first mentioned in local records in the sixteenth century. A short distance from the house the Regent's Canal joins the river Thames.

The next bend in the river brings the explorer to the Isle of Dogs, which contains a great many places of refreshment within its bounds. The Isle acquired its strange name because the royal dogs from the palace of Greenwich, across the river from the Island Gardens, were kept here, away from their royal owners, who doubtless wanted to enjoy quiet nights undisturbed by the noise of the dogs howling. Enter the Isle by West Ferry Road and you will find the **City Arms** (28) on the right-hand side of the road. Decorated in modern style, its great attraction, apart from its beer, is the metal sculpture of the Great Fire of London.

Continuing down the road, and regrettably having to pass several public houses on the way, you reach the junction of West Ferry Road and East Ferry Road. Here turn right and then almost immediately left into Ferry Street and find the **Ferry House** (29). It is a reminder of the ferry that used to carry passengers and horses across the Thames from Greenwich to the Isle of Dogs before the Greenwich Foot Tunnel was built in 1902. The nearby steps to the river are still called Horse Ferry Steps. From here it is a short walk to the Island Gardens, from where there is a fine view across the river to Greenwich and the Royal Naval College, Greenwich Park and the Queen's House.

Shortly afterwards you come to Glengarnock Avenue and the **Waterman's Arms** (30) with its splendid Edwardian decor and fine collection of items connected with old-time music halls. Collectors' pieces from the famous Collins Music Hall on Islington Green in north London were brought here, as were many other objects from the good old days of live theatre and variety shows in the nineteenth and early twentieth centuries.

It is hardly surprising to find the **Cubitt Arms** (31) on the Isle of Dogs, for many of the buildings were the work of Thomas Cubitt, the noted nineteenth-century speculative builder.

The Gun (32) in Cold Harbour, Poplar, brings to an end our search along the northern bank of the river Thames for inns and taverns of historical interest. It makes an ideal place from which to watch the traffic on the river. It is situated at the entrance to the West India Dock, but the earliest reference to the house is in the fifteenth century, long before the dock was built. Lady Hamilton owned a cottage in this then rural area, and Lord Nelson is said to have stayed at the Gun while courting her. An enclosed staircase houses a smuggler's spy-hole, and was often used during the Napoleonic Wars.

6
Meat market and thirsty porters

We start this tour of hostelries in High Holborn close to its junction with Gray's Inn Road. A public house was first established here in 1430 and from 1695 until 1984 it was Henekey's Wine House in Holborn. It has now been taken over by Samuel Smith's brewery and renamed the **Cittie of Yorke** (1). The present building has extensive cellars, which were put to good use as shelters in the times of the anti-Catholic Gordon Riots of the eighteenth century. Dickens has David Copperfield in temporary residence in the gate-house to Gray's Inn, next door to the tavern. A triangular fireplace in the centre of the room appears to have no chimney: the smoke escapes from the fireplace by way of a chimney under the floor. If you want to show your prowess at drinking there is a yard-glass at your disposal. It holds $3^3/4$ pints (2.13 litres) and all you have to do is to drink the contents down in one go without pausing for breath or spilling any on the floor.

Turn left outside the Cittie of Yorke and walk along the road towards the City of London, whose boundary is marked here, at Holborn Bars, by dragons holding the coat of arms of the City between their paws; this was the place where visitors to and from the City were checked and tolls were paid. It marks the limit of the jurisdiction of the Lord Mayor of London. Shortly after entering the City you will see the red brick building of the Prudential Assurance Company. At one corner of this is Leather Lane, whose street market attracts local residents and office workers every day from Mondays to Fridays.

Sitting on his horse, with his hat raised in the air, is Prince Albert, Queen Victoria's Prince Consort, said to be the politest statue in the whole of London. Here also is Hatton Garden, famous for its diamond merchants; and just to the side an old lamp-post points the way to the **Mitre** (2), Mitre Place. It takes its name from the headgear of a bishop and dates from 1547. It stands on land once owned by the Bishops of Ely, whose town house stood nearby. It is said that Queen Elizabeth I threatened to unfrock Bishop Richard Cox if he did not give the house and land to her favourite, Sir Christopher Hatton. In one corner of the bar there is a tree trunk said to be the remains of a cherry tree around which Elizabeth danced. At one time this tavern observed the licensing hours of Cambridgeshire and this was very convenient when they did not coincide with London hours. Even now the Mitre's hours are slightly different and it is best, in the evening, to check before you visit to make sure how long you have left for drinking!

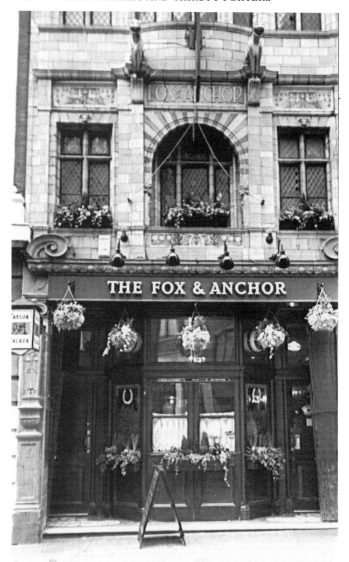

The Fox and Anchor, Charterhouse Street.

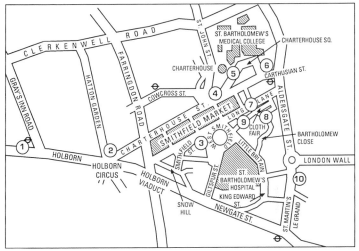

WALK 6: MEAT MARKET AND THIRSTY PORTERS

1. *The Cittie of Yorke*
2. *The Mitre*
3. *The Bishop's Finger*
4. *The Smithfield Tavern*
5. *The Fox and Anchor*
6. *The Sutton Arms*
7. *Ye Olde Red Cow*
8. *The Hand and Shears*
9. *The Rising Sun*
10. *The Raglan*

If you leave the Mitre and turn left you shortly enter Ely Place, which is a private road and not patrolled by the City police. Up to the Second World War a beadle walked the street after dark and called out the time and the condition of the weather for the benefit of anybody who happened to be awake. Returning through the wrought iron gates, turn left again and walk down Charterhouse Street until you reach the junction of Farringdon Road and Farringdon Street, between which the dragons of the City stand guard once more.

Cross the road in front of the dragons and walk up Charterhouse Street until West Poultry Avenue is reached. Walk along the avenue to the street called West Smithfield. Turn left and shortly reach the West Smithfield open space with the **Bishop's Finger** (3) on the corner. More correctly the title is the Rutland Hotel but it acquired its nickname from the porters of the market. The clientele is a mixture of City office workers and the porters from the meat market. A previous custom of climbing up the columns has now ceased, much to the satisfaction of the landlord. A painting over the bar shows Smithfield in 1912. Compare it with the market of today.

One of the largest meat markets in the world, Smithfield is built on land that was once the open 'smooth field' outside the wall of the City of London. Fairs regularly took place there, including the great St Bartholomew's Fair held each year until the late nineteenth century, when it was stopped because it had become too unruly. Cross West Smithfield and by way of Grand Avenue return to Charterhouse Street.

Here is the **Smithfield Tavern** (4), whose sign clearly shows the dress of a meat porter with his long smock-like overcoat and his flat-topped hat.

Next to the tavern, in the little side road that leads to the beautifully peaceful Charterhouse Square, is the **Fox and Anchor** (5). Before entering read the notice on the outside regarding the 'market holden at Smithfield'. In 1984 this Grade II listed building received an accolade for serving 'London's best breakfast'.

When the local Charterhouse monastery was dissolved in the reign of Henry VIII the property was bought by Thomas Sutton, a lawyer who had a passion for travel. He later became Elizabeth I's Master of Ordnance in the North, made a fortune from coalmining

Ye Olde Red Cow, Long Lane.

in Durham and founded Charterhouse School. The **Sutton Arms** (6) in Carthusian Street is a reminder of his benevolence.

A short walk away is Long Lane; John Stow wrote that it was 'truly long'. Here is **Ye Olde Red Cow** (7), a pleasant small nineteenth-century building, frequented by the thirsty porters of the market. A painting in the Guildhall shows the pub as it appeared in 1854. It once had a reputation for its hot toddy, popular with stage personalities who used the house.

From beside the Olde Red Cow a short lane leads to Cloth Fair and the **Hand and Shears** (8), where a tavern was first licensed in 1552. Here the Court of Piepowder (dusty feet) was held and the stallholders from the nearby market and fairs could settle their differences of opinion. Weights and measures used at the market were brought here to be tested. Offenders and fraudulent traders were fined or otherwise dealt with in accordance with the law of the times. Here, too, came the Lord Mayor of London to declare open the famous Smithfield fair by cutting the first piece of cloth to be sold. From this custom comes the present-day practice of cutting a piece of tape or cord when declaring open a new bridge, road or building. The traders, however, usually managed to start the proceedings themselves in an entirely different way the night before in the many taverns in the area.

At the other end of Cloth Fair is the **Rising Sun** (9), described as being 'another house of long standing that has jogged along for many years in a quiet way'. It has now been fully restored to its nineteenth-century grandeur.

After walking the entire length of Little Britain, you will reach Aldersgate, at the far end of which is the **Raglan** (10). It occupies one of the oldest hostelry sites in the City of London; Shakespeare knew the previous house well during his stay in London in the sixteenth century. Originally known as the Bush, it was changed to the Mourning Bush after the execution of Charles I by its Royalist landlord, who also painted the inn-sign black. After the Crimean War of the nineteenth century it was once again renamed — this time after the Commander-in-Chief of the British forces, Lord Raglan. Its cellars survive from the original house and incorporate parts of the old Roman wall and the city gate of Aldersgate.

The Chequers, Duke Street.

7
Up west around the 'Dilly

A piccadill was a collar ruff made in the seventeenth century, and a certain tailor who sold piccadills at his shop in the Haymarket built himself a house nearby and called it Piccadilly Hall. The place was described as being 'a fair house for entertainment and gaming, with handsome gravel walks, and an upper and lower bowling green', and it gave its name to the street in which it stood.

South of Piccadilly is the Haymarket, off which is Norris Street, where on the corner with St Alban's Street is the **Captain's Cabin** (1). The house has long been a meeting place of sailors and maritime folk. It became a home from home for many an Allied mariner during the Second World War and is still held in high esteem by them all. In the Captain's Log are written their names and comments: 'Home was never like this', 'It's great to be back again', and so on. The downstairs bar is the Captain's Cabin, complete with portholes, while the main deck (ground floor) has artefacts from the sea — a diver's helmet, figurehead, and so on. After leaving the Cabin, walk through to Regent Street, where on the left-hand side is Jermyn Street.

Off Jermyn Street is Babmaes Street; the name is a corruption of Baptist May, who, according to Samuel Pepys, was Charles II's 'court pimp' and received land here for his services. Here is the **Three Crowns** (2). Quite whose crowns they are is not stated. The street being a cul-de-sac, the house provides a quiet place for a drink either at lunchtime or on the way home.

Continue down Jermyn Street until St James's church, Piccadilly, appears on the right-hand side. Opposite the church is Duke of York Street. At number 2 is the **Red Lion** (3), a fine example of the nineteenth-century 'gin palace', with its mirrored walls and cast-iron spiral staircase leading from the bar.

Return to Jermyn Street, continue away from the church and turn left into Duke Street, St James's. Here is the **Chequers** (4) public house, but before entering look up at the inn-sign showing the Prime Minister's country house in Buckinghamshire, Chequers. The previous sign showed the familiar chequered board used for draughts or chess. Both these games were popular with people who frequented alehouses and the sign was also used by money changers.

Also in this street is the **Barley Mow** (5), with its Georgian features, copper pots, kettles and horse brasses. It was once connected to the house of the Japanese ambassador.

By this time the drinker may welcome a short walk in search of the next pub. Return to Jermyn Street again and walk along to Bury

Street. At the other end of this street are King Street and the **Golden Lion** (6), opposite Christie's, the auctioneers. It is a good place to recover after a visit to the saleroom across the road.

Diagonally opposite is the old Crown Alley. Walking down this alley is like stepping back in time, for it is a charming eighteenth-century back-street: on the right-hand side are small shops with shutters and iron bars to keep them secure when the staff have gone home. At the end of the alley stands the **Red Lion** (7), once described as the former alehouse standing in Crown Alley. But the gardens mentioned in the original lease of the building have disappeared, nor is there any sign of the secret passages that are said to link the tavern with the nearby St James's Palace. Perhaps these were the reason why it is called Crown Alley. A king might have used the place for a rendezvous with a mistress, and Charles II's mistress, Nell Gwynne, did have a house nearby in Pall Mall.

The alley leads to Pall Mall, but by turning right the walker soon reaches St James's Street. At the other end is Bennet Street, in which is the **Blue Posts** (8). The place is mentioned by the Restora-

(Left) The Goat Tavern, Stafford Street.

(Right) The Blue Posts, Bennet Street.

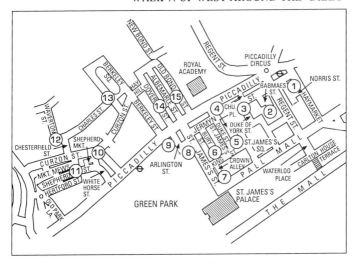

WALK 7: UP WEST AROUND THE 'DILLY

tion dramatist George Etheridge in 1677 as an alehouse from where blue-coloured sedan chairs could be hired. Posts, also painted blue, were to be found in the old courtyard here at the side of the horse troughs, and it is from these that the public house, rebuilt after being bombed in the Second World War, was named. Inside the house the publican keeps, as a showpiece, one of the blue sedan chairs; but it is not for hire or sale!

Arlington Street, to the side of the public house, leads to Piccadilly and the **Ritz Hotel** (9), which has licensed bars, where those who would like a change from drinking in public bars may enjoy the quiet seclusion of the hotel. (Only hotel residents will be served with drink after the licensing hours.) When an attempt was made to pull down the hotel and redevelop the site protests were made, and the hotel is now a protected building and cannot be altered externally, although improvements may be made to the rooms.

It is a short walk down Piccadilly to Half Moon Street, at the end of which are Curzon Street and **Ye Grapes** (10), nestling in the corner of Shepherd Market. It was built as the Market Coffee House in 1736 when Edward Shepherd was developing the area, the site of the once notorious May Fair, with shops and houses. Although grapes were sold in the market and fair, the inn-sign was

Ye Grapes, Curzon Street.

originally used to denote a wine house as opposed to an ale or beer house.

Diagonally opposite the Grapes is the **Shepherd** public house (11), named after the founder of Shepherd Market. Inside the house is a sedan chair, now used as a telephone kiosk, that was once owned, and doubtless sat in, by George II's son the Duke of Cumberland. There is also a collection of Chinese porcelain in the bar. The attractive exterior of the building is in Georgian style with light green and gold offsetting the bottle glazing of the small bow windows, making this an eighteenth-century pub with a difference.

The **Red Lion** (12) in Waverton Street is as old as the Shepherd, both having been built in the mid eighteenth century. It has been described as a country house in the heart of London and one hundred years ago it was a farmhouse. A pair of Dick Turpin's pistols is on show in the bar.

From the Red Lion walk along Charles Street and at the far end of the street, at the junction with Hay's Mews, is the **I Am the Only Running Footman** (13). The job of this servant was to run ahead of his master's coach to warn the tollkeepers of the impending approach of the coach, pay the necessary toll and then to hurry on to the next tollgate. In the seventeenth and eighteenth centuries the strength and endurance of these servants of the aristocracy was prodigious: it is recorded that they could run between sixteen and twenty miles in little over two hours. The running footman carried in his hand his wand of office, which contained his refreshment consisting of red wine and the white of eggs mixed together to sustain him in his often long and tedious journeys. There is no other public house similarly named.

Cross the southern side of Berkeley Square, walk up Hay Hill into Dover Street and turn right. On the next corner, on the left-hand side of the street, is the **Duke of Albemarle** (14). Inside there is an original street-name sign reading 'This is Stafford Street 1686'. Although there has been a house on this site since that time the present building dates from the twentieth century. The Duke is also commemorated in the nearby street that bears his name. He was granted the land by the grateful monarch, Charles II, at the restoration of the monarchy in 1660, but the area was laid out by Sir Thomas Bond.

Further along Stafford Street is the **Goat Tavern** (15), with a life-size goat as its inn-sign. In 1736 a trust was set up here for the benefit of the needy of the two local parishes. Rent is still paid to this fund.

To return to Piccadilly from the Goat, turn right outside the house, walk along to Albemarle Street, then turn left and down to Piccadilly.

The Grenadier, Wilton Row.

8
Belgravia and South-west One

From Hyde Park Corner, the **Grenadier** (1) in Wilton Row can be approached either along Knightsbridge, turning left into Wilton Place, and left again into Wilton Crescent, after which it is the first on the left, or from Grosvenor Crescent, which runs by the side of the Lanesborough Hotel; turn into Wilton Crescent and find Wilton Row on the right. Here the Duke of Wellington stabled his horses and there is a mounting block supposed to have been used by him. Appropriately the theme of the tavern is military (Old Barrack Yard is close by) and the house is haunted by an officer of the Grenadiers who was caught cheating at cards. The Grenadier is one of the most charming refreshment houses in Belgravia.

Return to Grosvenor Crescent and turn right towards Belgrave Square. This land was reclaimed from marsh by Viscount Belgrave, a member of the Grosvenor family. (Belgrave is a small hamlet on the family's estates near Chester.) Much of the soil used for this work came from the newly dug docks of east London. Cross the square by the side leading directly out of the Crescent to reach Chapel Street on the left-hand side. Enter this street and you will come to Groom Place. The **Horse and Groom** (2) is a delightful nineteenth-century house. It is hard to think of the area once being associated with lepers and a hospital, the Lock Hospital, for ladies of easy virtue who had contracted 'the dreaded disease'. Stables were often found at the rear of the elegant houses of the fashionable squares of the eighteenth century, and in them were horses and grooms — hence the pub's name.

Directly in front of the Horse and Groom the mews leads to Chester Street, and, by turning to the right, to Belgrave Square. Walk along the side of the square to Chesham Place, off which is Belgrave Mews West. Here is to be found the **Star** (3), 'one of the handsomest pubs in London', a title that it justifies, both inside and out. The clientele comprises gamblers (who are always good for a hot tip), actors and directors (film and financial), alongside plain-clothes policemen and photographers. It is not a place to take an elderly relative.

On leaving the mews return to Chesham Place, turn right and walk along to Lyall Street, then turn left to Eaton Square. Turn right along Eaton Gate and walk to Eaton Terrace. At number 22 is the **Antelope** (4), built in 1827 mainly for the use of the servants in the big houses nearby. The local inhabitants no longer employ house-maids, footmen or butlers and the pub's regulars now include many rugby players.

Return to Eaton Square and turn right into Elizabeth Street, two streets away from Eaton Terrace; at number 44 is the **Prince of Wales** (5). In the nineteenth century the tavern was a popular meeting place for the coachmen of the neighbourhood, who doubtless liked to get away from their lords and masters and to exchange gossip about them. The building was redeveloped in 1972 and is now mock Tudor in style.

At the other end of Elizabeth Street is Buckingham Palace Road. Here at number 56 is the **Victoria** (6), a spacious and very traditionally styled drinking place. On leaving, turn left and walk to Victoria Street. Turn right.

In Allington Street (a turn to the left) is the **Stage Door** (7), a Dickensian-style pub that gets its name from the Victoria Palace Theatre on the opposite side of the street. The front of the house is painted a sombre black but it is highlighted with window boxes, and there are pavement tables and chairs. Inside there is a quiet intimate atmosphere created by the use of screens and seating in cubicles. The bric-à-brac around the place is theatrical. It is a good place to pop out to during the interval in the show at the theatre.

On the corner of Allington Street and Victoria Street stands the **Duke of York** (8). The interior is designed in the traditional wooden-beamed style. Being adjacent to the Victoria Palace Theatre, it

The Colonies, Wilfred Street.

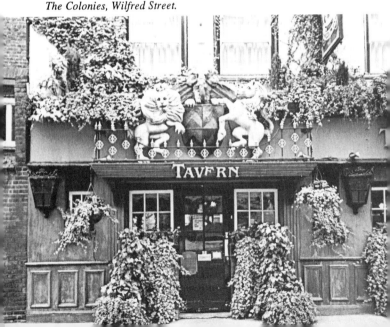

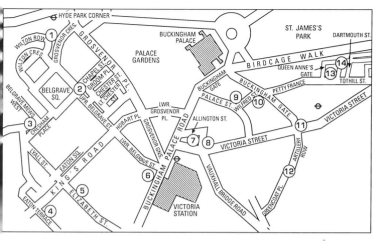

WALK 8: BELGRAVIA AND SOUTH-WEST ONE

counts among its many clients theatregoers as well as local office workers.

From Allington Street it is a short walk along Victoria Street to Palace Street, where on the corner of Wilfred Street is the **Cask and Glass** (9), a friendly nineteenth-century pub whose exterior looks like a little doll's house. It is covered with floral displays throughout the year. Inside the ceiling is low and the welcome is warm.

The **Colonies** (10) in Wilfred Street should not be missed. Built in the colonial style, it is decorated with animal skins and trophies from the golden days of the British Empire.

At the end of Wilfred Street is Buckingham Gate and where the latter joins Victoria Street stands the **Albert** (11). Although its future was once in great doubt, it has defied progress and survived the redevelopment of the area. In more leisured times they served large English breakfasts here. Prince Albert, consort of Queen Victoria, looks down from the signboard. Downstairs the gas lighting has recently been restored and the first-floor room is dominated by portraits of two other great Victorians, Disraeli and Gladstone.

In the days of charity schools the children who attended them were distinguished by the colour of their coats. Blue, grey and

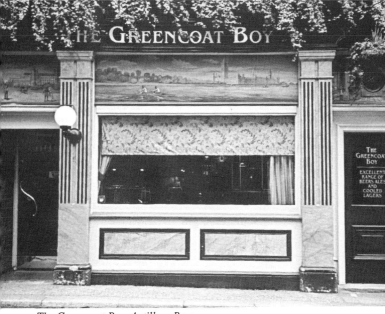

The Greencoat Boy, Artillery Row.

green coats were to be found in this area, and although only the Grey Coat Hospital (school) survives today, the **Greencoat Boy** (12), at the end of Artillery Row, off Victoria Street, is remembered in the public house that bears his name. The façade is decorated above the window with attractive murals of Victorian scenes.

A short walk away, across Victoria Street, up Palmer Street (to the right of the Albert), and right along Petty France, is **number 9 Queen Anne's Gate** (13). This has in its basement a number of items from public houses destroyed in the Second World War. The relics were gathered together by John Betjeman, Poet Laureate, John Piper the artist, and Hubert de Cronin Hastings, owner of the Architectural Press. This is a public house without a licence to sell alcoholic drinks.

At the end of the same street, where it joins Dartmouth Street, is the **Two Chairmen** (14). It seems quite natural that the Two Chairmen should be found in an area of eighteenth-century elegance. With a little imagination one can still picture a lord and lady arriving at one of the beautiful houses of Queen Anne's Gate or enjoying themselves at the nearby cockpit while their sedan-chair attendants waited for them in the tavern.

From here it is a short walk by way of Queen Anne's Gate to St James's Park station.

9
Drinking by the Thames's south side

In chapter 5 we visited the interesting taverns on the north bank of the Thames. This tour describes those on the south bank, starting at Mortlake in the west and finishing at Greenwich in the east.

Commanding a fine view of the finishing line of the annual Oxford and Cambridge Boat Race, the **Ship** (1) at Mortlake (reached from Ship Lane off Lower Richmond Road) dates back to the time of Elizabeth I, although the present building was erected during the reign of George I in the eighteenth century. Shown on the maps as the Hart's Horn, it became the Blue Anchor in the seventeenth century, before adopting its present name in the nineteenth century. There is evidence of a ford across the river nearby, and doubtless this was a good place to refresh oneself before or after crossing the river.

From the Ship return to the main road and turn left. It leads to the riverside towpath and to the **White Hart** (2), with its pleasant Victorian exterior. It is situated on a great curve of the river, and from the house a splendid view of the Oxford and Cambridge Boat Race can be obtained.

Pass under the Barnes railway bridge, still keeping along the riverside, to reach the **Bull's Head** public house (3). Standing on the site of a farmhouse owned by a family from the north of England, the Lowthers, the family of the Earls of Lonsdale, the present building was erected in the nineteenth century. At that time the inn was a coaching station, and the stables have been converted into a

The White Hart, Mortlake.

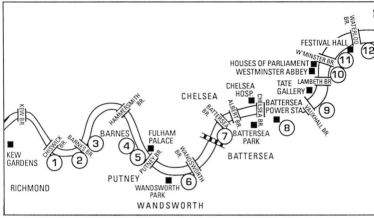

WALK 9: DRINKING BY THE THAMES'S SOUTH SIDE

restaurant; many of the old fittings have been retained and incorporated in the decor. Popular pub games, such as darts, shove-halfpenny and dominoes, contribute to the atmosphere of the place.

The start of the Boat Race course is at Putney, where there are two establishments by the riverside, before reaching Putney Bridge. The **Duke's Head** (4), from whose riverside bar the full sweep of the river can be admired, has an inn-sign showing a duke wearing the riband and star of the Most Noble Order of St Michael and St George, but without identifying him by name.

Next door is the **Star and Garter** (5), which contains memories of races won and lost. Its greatest prize is a pewter tankard that was washed up on the riverbank by the former Surrey Dock in 1951. It bears the inscription 'Star and Garter, Putney, 1750'.

At the foot of Wandsworth Bridge are Jews Row and the **Ship** (6), with its two bars filled with photographs of warships and wrecks, and even a large model ship. The garden terrace runs down to the river steps where river craft can tie up.

Standing at the foot of West London railway bridge, which is south-west of Battersea bridge, and incorporated in a modern block of flats is the **Chandler** (7). On the side wall can be seen the coat of arms of the Worshipful Company of Tallow Chandlers of the City of London. The signboard shows a ship's chandler with a back-

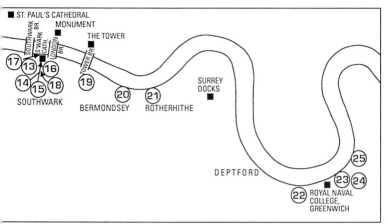

ground of several fine sailing ships. The riverside terrace overlooks the river and the river walk that leads to the eighteenth-century parish church of St Mary. There are several house-boats moored along this stretch of the river.

Beyond Battersea Park, and shortly after the railway bridge in Nine Elms Lane, Thessaly Road will be found on the right-hand side. A few hundred yards along it is the **Butchers Arms** (8), displaying the coat of arms of the Worshipful Company of Butchers of the City of London. The interior decoration consists of butchers' knives and cleavers, creating an atmosphere appropriate to the name.

Just beyond the complex new road junction at Vauxhall Cross, near Vauxhall railway station, the road becomes the Albert Embankment, another reminder of the Prince Consort of Queen Victoria, and here stands the **Old Father Thames** (9). The Old Red Cow that once stood on this site has gone and in its place this far more sophisticated house has been built. It has a commanding view of the river from the Tate Gallery to the Houses of Parliament and its neighbour is the London Fire Brigade headquarters, and so the pub receives the attention that it deserves.

After the roundabout by Lambeth Bridge, the roadway becomes Lambeth Palace Road, passing first the former church of St Mary-at-Lambeth, now the home of the Museum of Garden History, and

The Ship, Mortlake.

next the gatehouse of Lambeth Palace, the London home of the Archbishop of Canterbury, with its magnificent Tudor towers.

At the junction with Westminster Bridge Road, beside the modern extension of County Hall, is the **Florence Nightingale** (10), formerly called the Pill Box and later the Geoffrey Chaucer. Today it commemorates the 'Lady of the Lamp', whose name is permanently associated with nursing in the Crimean War and whose statue is on the terrace of St Thomas's Hospital, between Lambeth Palace Road and the river.

Aptly renamed during 1977, the year of the Silver Jubilee of Queen Elizabeth II, the **Jubilee** (11) in York Road was previously called the Ordnance Arms, after a small arms depot that used to be close by.

By the side of Blackfriars Bridge is the **Doggett's Coat and Badge** (12), part of a riverside development. It is an appropriate name for a splendid site. Thomas Doggett was an Irish comedian who came to live in London in the latter part of the seventeenth century. He instituted the race now called Doggett's Coat and Badge to commemorate the accession to the throne of George I. It is rowed over a course of 4½ miles (7.25 km) from Chelsea to London Bridge towards the end of July each year. The winner receives a scarlet coat and silver badge. The decoration of the house includes a life-size figure of the coat and badge, while on the walls are displayed paintings of the barges of the City livery companies.

The way to the next public house takes us through a most interesting part of south London — Bankside. After leaving the Doggett's Coat and Badge cross Blackfriars Bridge Road, go down some steps and keep left to the riverside, passing the former Bankside Power Station, then a house with a plaque declaring that Sir Christopher Wren lived there and then the complex of the replica Globe Theatre. Pass under Southwark Bridge, once a toll bridge but now freed from tolls by the City of London which owns it, and so reach the **Anchor** (13). It was once surrounded by warehouses, but there has been much redevelopment in the area. The present building, rebuilt in the seventeenth century, replaces the one patronised by William Shakespeare, whose Globe Theatre was just round the corner in Park Street. With a glass of Empress of Russia stout, which is a mixture of ale, beer and twopenny (a pale, small beer first brewed in eighteenth-century London, of lesser gravity than other beers, and costing two pence a pint), one can imagine the inn when it was used

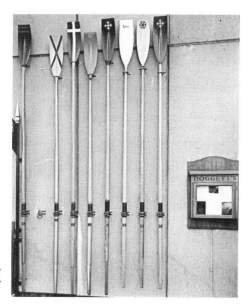

The Doggett's Coat and Badge, near Blackfriars Bridge.

The George Inn, Borough High Street.

by rivermen or by warders from the nearby Clink prison. Tales are
told of the notorious press gangs who raided the house looking for
young men to force to join the Royal Navy. The roadway that once
ran in front of the Anchor has been removed and the forecourt has
been redeveloped so that customers can eat and drink while watching the river flow by.

Now go under the railway arches opposite the Anchor and follow Clink Street between warehouses to Cathedral Street, which leads beside the Borough Market, one of London's oldest markets. In the centre of the market stands the **Market Porter** (14), where open fireplaces, private booths and traditional timber decor welcome porters and visitors alike. Stoney Street runs along the other side of the market.

On the corner of Southwark Street and Stoney Street is the **Southwark Tavern** (15), a late Victorian pub on a historic site, that of the debtors' prison, whose cells are now a wine bar. There are many interesting prints and memorabilia on the walls.

Turn left to Borough High Street, cross over and turn right. The **George Inn** (16) lies back off the street in its own yard on your left-hand side. It is the last of the galleried coaching inns of London and shows its visitors some of the glory of coaching inns in the heyday of horse-drawn transport. During the seventeenth and eighteenth centuries coaches departed regularly from here to the villages around London. William Shakespeare and his fellow actors drank here as well as at the Anchor. John Stow, writing in the late sixteenth century, mentions documents, now in the Public Record Office, that contain the plans of the building of 1552; this house was destroyed by fire in 1677. The building that survives today replaced it, though part of it was destroyed at the beginning of the twentieth century when the railway companies needed extra room for their goods traffic. During the summer months companies of actors and actresses perform plays by Shakespeare on the loading bay, much as their forbears performed in the courtyards for the pleasure of the guests. Charles Dickens's Little Dorrit lived in nearby Marshalsea Prison and was married in the local church of St George; she wrote a letter to Clennam from the George. Dickens must have known the tavern well from visiting his father in the prison.

Return to the Borough High Street and walk back towards London Bridge. At the end of the bridge there is on the left-hand side a flight of steps that lead down to Montague Close, where, on the right, can be seen the **Mudlark** (17). The sign shows one of the children who in Victorian times would scavenge the foreshore of the river in search of coins and other treasures. Another form of 'mud-larking' was far more dangerous: it involved boys and men packing mud underneath barges in order to prevent them slipping from the side of the wharf while being unloaded. Pictures and prints on the walls show life in and around Southwark in the nineteenth century. Outside the building can be seen pieces of London Bridge that were left behind when the rest was sent to the USA some years ago. There are also drawings of the various bridges that have stood here, beginning with the Roman bridge.

Close by is St Mary Overie's Dock, an ancient landing place for goods for the citizens of Southwark. Here one of the nineteenth-century warehouses has been converted into the **Old Thameside Inn** (18). From the riverside terrace one can enjoy splendid views across to the City of London or watch the boats on the river pass by. The dock, where in former times citizens of Southwark were allowed to unload their goods free of tax, now houses the *Kathleen and May* wooden schooner.

Follow Tooley Street past London Bridge station until it crosses Tower Bridge Road. If you want to enjoy a drink or two surrounded by local history and old-time policemen, then the **Copper** (19) at number 206-8 Tower Bridge Road is the place to visit. 'Copper' is a slang word for a policeman; another is 'grasshopper'.

Tooley Street runs into Jamaica Road, which leads to Rotherhithe. In Rotherhithe Street hard by the riverside is the **Angel** (20); a fine view of the river and the City of London towards Tower Bridge can be had from the back rooms and balcony. Its original title was the Salutation, when it was kept by the monks of Bermondsey Abbey, but this was considered too religious and so after the Reformation its name was changed to the Angel, although doubtless the Angel was the angel of the Salutation of the Blessed Virgin Mary, and the inn has retained this title ever since the sixteenth century. It is built on piles over the river and there are trapdoors in the floor that must have proved very useful to the river pirates and smugglers, who could thus enter and leave the house without being seen. Samuel Pepys, Secretary to the Navy Office in the seventeenth century, records in his diary that he visited the inn. Captain Cook visited the Angel long before he discovered Australia.

At the junction of Rotherhithe Street and St Mary Church Street stands the **Mayflower** (21), which has been the centre of the life of the parish since the sixteenth century, when its name was the Shippe. In 1611 Captain Christopher Jones moored his ship, the *Mayflower*, close by the tavern. Doubtless the talk of the tavern in those days was the news of the New World across the Atlantic and the founding of the colonies in America. Some ten years later, when the *Mayflower* returned to home waters, the captain was taken ill and died at Rotherhithe. He is buried in the parish church near two of his partners, John Moore and Richard Gardener. The restored tavern today recreates the atmosphere of the seventeenth century and is said to incorporate parts of the *Mayflower* within its structure. It was one of the very few inns licensed to sell postage stamps, American ones as well as British because of its close associations with the United States. The jetty commands a fine view of the river and is a very pleasant place to sit and watch the river and the boats.

The former fishing village of Greenwich has some interesting

Trafalgar Tavern, Greenwich.

public houses nestling around the parish church, naval college and the great open space of Greenwich Park. Hard by the *Cutty Sark*, one of the last and most famous clipper ships of the nineteenth century, is the **Gypsy Moth** (22), dedicated to the late Sir Francis Chichester, the lone round-the-world yachtsman. His boat, *Gypsy Moth IV*, is close to the *Cutty Sark*. Inside the pub can be seen pictures of his yacht as well as a map plotting his route on his famous voyage. The signboard shows the Gypsy Moth aircraft that Sir Francis flew, as well as his yacht which he named after it.

Standing on the site of the former George public house is the **Trafalgar Tavern** (23), rebuilt in 1837 and renamed in honour of the great sea battle won by Lord Nelson in 1805. In between times the building has been used by the nearby Royal Naval College as living quarters, as a home for old seamen and from 1915 to 1965 as a men's club, known as the Royal Alfred Aged Merchant Seamen's Institute. At its restoration it reverted to the name of Trafalgar Tavern. Members of Parliament used to meet here for 'Ministerial Whitebait Dinners' during the summer Parliamentary recess, a time when whitebait was in season. Whitebait are no longer caught in the river Thames off Greenwich but, in season, the dish appears on the menu of the tavern. A founder member of the Institute of British Architects and Secretary of the Architects Club, Joseph Kay, designed the present building while he was Surveyor of Greenwich Hospital. The tavern was mentioned by Charles Dickens in *Our Mutual Friend*.

Almost next door to the Trafalgar Tavern is the **Yacht** (24), which has stood here for at least three hundred years. The Greenwich meridian line runs through the building. Many tales have been told about the house since the first Queen Elizabeth sailed by to enjoy the comfort of Greenwich Palace, where she was born and for which she had a lifelong affection. From the modern extension to the building, customers can watch the river traffic.

The **Cutty Sark** (25) was the Union, Ballast Quay, at the end of Pelton Road, when the maps of the nineteenth century were drawn, and even then it had been there for over two hundred years. Now it has been renamed in honour of the great clipper ship, the *Cutty Sark*, which stands in the dry dock on the other side of the Royal Naval College. The house was first built in the seventeenth century, when from the upper windows fine views could be had over the river, both towards to the spreading dockland and to the open marshes of the other bank. Private quayside seating provides a pleasant place to rest and enjoy the view. Inside, a mysterious former seaman makes his presence known by unscrewing the lids of jars and distributing their contents around the bar — but never during opening hours.

The Yacht, Greenwich.

10
Pretty Polly Perkins land

Whether Polly Perkins really lived in Paddington Green and was wooed by the milkman need not concern us too much as we walk in search of a few pleasant houses in this historic area of London, but we start to the west of it, in Inverness Terrace, off the Bayswater Road near Queensway underground station.

Edward VII brought his mistress, Lily Langtry, to Inverness Terrace and **Inverness Court** (1) and wooed her here. He had a theatre built for her within the house, where she could perform and entertain him and his friends. Today the house is a hotel functioning both as a tavern and as an inn, for there is a public bar and one can both eat and sleep here if one wishes.

Further down the Bayswater Road is the **Swan** (2) established in 1775. It stands on part of the site once occupied by Sir John Hill's physic garden, a popular place of entertainment in the eighteenth century, but no serious rival to Vauxhall or Cremorne Gardens. In later years it became the Floral Tea Gardens and was painted by Paul Sandby; a watercolour in the British Museum print room shows the unspoilt rural appearance of Paddington parish at that time. In another painting Sandby shows two low tiled buildings, in front of which are a wooden fence and a small drinking trough, and a bridge over the Westbourne river nearby. The house still retains much of its charm, and its forecourt makes a pleasant gathering place for locals and visitors during the summer months.

Beyond Lancaster Gate station turn left into Westbourne Street to reach Bathurst Street on the right. In the reign of George III the **Archery Tavern** in Bathurst Street (3) supplied refreshment not only to the people who lived nearby but also, in the early nineteenth century, to members of the Royal Toxophilite Society — the archers. There must have been considerable open space here then for the archers to practise in the fields around the house. The original stables and courtyard of the old inn have long since disappeared, although there are stables with horses for hire in the mews behind the public house. After relinquishing their land here, the Royal Toxophilite Society moved their butts to Regent's Park until early in the twentieth century, when they returned to south Paddington and used the former burial ground of St George's, Hanover Square, in the Bayswater Road. But that site was sold and flats and garages were built on it, so the society once more left the district. Bathurst Street leads to Sussex Square, at the opposite corner of which go left along Stanhope Terrace to Strathearn Place.

At the end of Strathearn Place stands the **Victoria** (4), with its

The Swan, Bayswater Road.

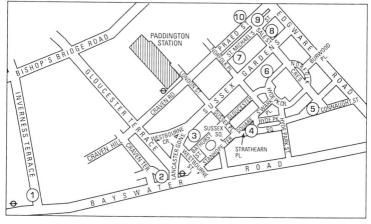

WALK 10: PRETTY POLLY PERKINS LAND
1. *The Inverness Court*
2. *The Swan*
3. *The Archery Tavern*
4. *The Victoria*
5. *The Duke of Kendal*
6. *The Monkey Puzzle*
7. *The Sir Alexander Fleming*
8. *The Royal Exchange*
9. *The Great Western*
10. *The Grand Junction Arms*

reconstructed bar from the old Gaiety Theatre in the Strand and its distinctive Victorian decor. The restaurant is Our Mutual Friend, and one likes to think of Dickens, who at one time lived in the Bayswater Road nearby, visiting the place as his local. In a restoration a few years ago a painting came to light which, after having been carefully cleaned, was revealed to be of a past member of the royal family; it was presented to Her Majesty the Queen and now forms part of the royal portrait collection.

Follow the right-hand side of Hyde Park Square to Connaught Street. Opened in the 1820s, the **Duke of Kendal** (5), at the junction of Connaught Street with Kendal Street, is dedicated to Prince Leopold, Duke of Kendal, whose marriage to Crown Princess Charlotte connected him with the British royal family. He later became the first king of the Belgians, and Queen Victoria's favourite uncle. Because the house stands at an oblique junction of two roads the bar is triangular.

In the 1960s much of south Paddington was redeveloped: the grand old houses of the nineteenth century were torn down by the landowners, the Church Commissioners, and new high-rise flats have taken their place. During this time several nineteenth-century public houses were demolished and not replaced.

The Archery Tavern , Bathurst Street.

Sussex Gardens, previously called Grand Junction Road and the New Road, was part of London's first official bypass, originally formed in the eighteenth century as a route for the animals going to Smithfield. Today the **Monkey Puzzle** (6) is to be found there, complete with its monkey puzzle tree, or Chile pine, in the forecourt. It replaced the Mitre, which stood where Devonport Flats now stand. The Mitre was an appropriate name as much of the land in Paddington was owned by the Bishops of London.

One must visit the little back streets between Sussex Gardens and Praed Street to find the **Sir Alexander Fleming** (7). It is in St Michael's Street on the corner with Bouverie Place. The inn-sign shows Sir Alexander Fleming, whose discovery of penicillin in the nearby St Mary's Hospital, Praed Street, made him famous. The house is frequented by students from the local medical school.

(Left) Our Mutual Friend restaurant at the Victoria, Strathearn Place.

A favourite quotation from Shakespeare's play *Richard III* appears on the inn-sign of the **Royal Exchange** (8), on the corner of Sale Place and St Michael's Street. The sign shows the king, on his knees, offering the crown of England to a country yokel with the most feeble-looking horse that can be imagined, while above the picture the words 'A horse, a horse, my kingdom for a horse' explain its significance.

Being near the terminus of the Great Western Railway at Paddington station, Praed Street has a number of railway taverns; the one on the corner of Sale Place, the **Great Western** (9), shows on its two signs steam locomotives of the former GWR, in the livery of the company, reminding visitors of the glorious days of the railways, before electricity and diesel took over from coal and steam.

Nearby is the **Grand Junction Arms** (10), which was built earlier in the twentieth century in the 'black and white' style of the sixteenth century. It is a reminder of the closeness of the house to the Paddington Basin, which is an arm of the Grand Union Canal, the canal being an amalgamation of the Grand Junction and Regent's Canals. One of the spokesmen for the Grand Union Canal Act was William Praed, who gives his name to the street. Note the grotesque stone figures that support the roofline on the outside of the building.

The Sir Alexander Fleming, St Michael's Street.

(Above) The Kings Arms, Poland Street.
(Below left) The Crown and Two Chairmen, Dean Street.
(Below right) The Nellie Dean, Dean Street.

11
Happy hunting ground —
Soho and beyond

The word *soho* was the password at the battle of Sedgemoor in 1685, the last major battle fought on English soil; it was the English equivalent of the French hunting cry of 'tally-ho', but it has today come to mean the area of London bounded by Oxford Street, Charing Cross Road, Shaftesbury Avenue and Regent Street, which is full of restaurants, clubs, pubs and small shops.

Leave Piccadilly Circus by way of Glasshouse Street, passing the Regent Palace Hotel. Walk on to Brewer Street, to the **Crown** (1), a house much frequented by Charles Dickens and mentioned in his book *Nicholas Nickleby*, in which Newman Noggs is 'always found or heard of at the Crown'.

Walk along Brewer Street until Lexington Street appears on the left, and walk the entire length of that street to reach Broadwick Street and the **John Snow** (2). It was formerly called the Newcastle-on-Tyne, presumably from a former owner's connections with that city, but the title deeds only go back to 1927. Information posted on the walls of the bars recalls how in the nineteenth century a local doctor called John Snow traced an outbreak of cholera to the pump here and persuaded the vestry to remove the handle in order to prevent the local inhabitants from using the well while it was contaminated. Further examination revealed that the brickwork of a drain under number 40 was defective and sewage was seeping into the source of the water supply.

It was a former inn, the King of Poland, that gave its name to Poland Street, which leads from Broadwick Street to Oxford Street. At number 23 is the **Kings Arms** (3), the original arms being those of James II: the stained glass windows display the lion of Scotland and the fleur-de-lis of France. During the eighteenth century a meeting took place here which led to the revival of the Ancient Order of Druids in Britain. Dating from pre-Roman times, the Druids combined priestly, judicial and political functions. Their origins are obscure, but the movement spread throughout Europe and across the Atlantic to America. The name 'Druid' may mean 'oak', and oak trees grew in abundance here until the seventeenth century, when many of the streets were laid out by Gregory King.

Leading to Berwick Street from Poland Street is D'Arblay Street, which takes its name from Madame D'Arblay, who, as Fanny Burney, spent part of her childhood near here. From here continue to Wardour Street, where at number 99 is the **Intrepid Fox** (4). Originally called 'the Crown' for no other reason than the fact that the landlord was an ardent royalist, it changed after Charles James Fox, the English liberal statesman, orator and champion of democratic government, adopted it as his drinking house. He 'used to sit quietly in the corner, pretending to be a Tory, with his wig pulled down over his eyes'. This is said to have so affected the landlord that he offered free beer on polling day for the 1784 general election. The house was crowded all day. Many of the film industry people who have their offices in Wardour Street use the Intrepid Fox as their 'local'.

Turn right in Wardour Street, then left along St Anne's Court, to reach Dean Street. In Dean Street is the **Nellie Dean** (5), complete with the good lady by the stream and the watermill of the famous song. However, the street name has nothing to do with Nellie Dean. The street was named after Dean Compton of the Chapel Royal, who later became Bishop of London in the seventeenth century and whose connections with the area are purely ecclesiastical.

Also in Dean Street is the **Crown and Two Chairmen** (6); it was so called because Queen Anne sat for her portrait by Sir James Thornhill in his studio opposite. Doubtless while the artist was at work with his painting the bearers of the Queen's sedan chair were busy in the public house opposite. At one time the tenant was Richard Moreland, who is supposed to have been the last landlord in London to wear a pigtail and top boots. Here George Sala first met Thackeray, and he records that he sang 'The Mahogany Tree' in the small club room over the bar.

Bateman Street by the side of the Crown leads to Frith Street and 'the only pub in Frith Street', the **Dog and Duck** (7). In the days of hunting in the area there would no doubt have been a pond or two where duck were to be found, and the dog was the means of retrieving the duck once it had been shot by the hunter.

Frith Street was the place from which John Logie Baird in 1926 transmitted the first television picture. A short walk north along it leads to Soho Square, in which stands the statue by Cibber of Charles II. From the square Sutton Row leads out into Charing Cross Road and so brings the walker to the very busy road junction with Tottenham Court Road and Oxford Street. At the end of Tottenham Court Road is the Dominion Theatre. The former Horseshoe Hotel was here, its site now occupied by Boots the Chemist. It was established in the seventeenth century, though it has been rebuilt completely since that time. There are two suggestions as to how it received its name. The first is that the brewery next door had a horseshoe nailed above the entrance doorway, and the second that once the main dining room had a horseshoe-shaped table. The brewery has long since disappeared along with the hotel and bar but when it was still in existence an enormous vat, said to hold 3,555

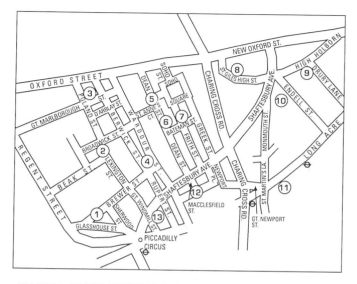

WALK 11: HAPPY HUNTING GROUND — SOHO AND BEYOND
1. The Crown
2. The John Snow
3. The Kings Arms
4. The Intrepid Fox
5. The Nellie Dean
6. The Crown and Two Chairmen
7. The Dog and Duck
8. The Café Munchen
9. The White Hart
10. The Cross Keys
11. The John Kemble
12. The De Hems
13. The Red Lion

barrels of liquid, burst its sides and poured out its contents over the neighbourhood. Eight people died as a result, either by drowning or by suffocation.

Many thieves, murderers and martyrs had reason to be thankful for the former White Lion, St Giles High Street (off New Oxford Street, to the right), now called **Café München** (8), because it was here that they received their last drink on earth, a draught of ale known as St Giles' Bowl, to fortify them on their journey to the gallows that stood at the junction of Tottenham Court Road and Oxford Street or further to the notorious Tyburn gallows, at what is now Marble Arch, which could be used to hang 24 people at once. Near this site in the seventeenth century a family contracted the plague, and neighbours, fearing that they too would catch the disease, moved to Westminster; from here, in turn, their neighbours moved into the City of London. So the Great Plague of 1665 started and spread, by the movement of families from one place to another.

Continue along St Giles High Street, cross Shaftesbury Avenue to High Holborn and walk along to the end of Drury Lane, where stands the **White Hart** (9), which was first licensed in the early thirteenth century and where in the seventeenth century Nell Gwynne is said to have stayed. This was one of a small number of inns where convicted criminals were given a drink while on their way to Tyburn Tree to be 'hanged, drawn and quartered'. It is on record that Jack Sheppard, the highwayman, had his last glass of beverage here in 1724.

Return along High Holborn and turn left into Endell Street. Here is the **Cross Keys** (10), which has been described as a 'high-class junk-shop', with plants in chamberpots, and 'an art gallery of fakes', with copies of paintings by such artists as Picasso and Matisse on display. They are all added attractions to the prints and drawings that hang on walls of the bars.

Endell Street leads to Long Acre, which forms the northern boundary of Covent Garden and the theatre district of the Strand, and here can be found the **John Kemble** public house (11). John Philip Kemble and his sister, Sarah Siddons, were stars of the London stage in the eighteenth century. John made his London debut at the Drury Lane Theatre in 1783 as Hamlet. He died in Switzerland and is buried in Lausanne. The decoration of the house comprises prints and pictures of theatres and of the great actor.

Head west along Long Acre to St Martin's Lane, continue along Great Newport Street to Charing Cross Road, turning right to Cambridge Circus, and there left into Shaftesbury Avenue, which forms the southern boundary of Soho. A turning off to the left is Macclesfield Street. Here is the **De Hems** (12) public house. *De Hems* is Dutch for 'windmill' and the theme of the decoration is Dutch, with copies of paintings by artists from Holland. This is one of the few drinking establishments in London where Dutch lager — *orangeboom* — can be found. The pub used to specialise in seafood and after a rare visit by Tolstoy in the nineteenth century he wrote:

Four and twenty oysters floating up the Thames

Finished as an oystershellabration at De Hems.

As it stands at the edge of the modern Chinatown, the house has an added attraction at the time of the Chinese New Year in late January or early February.

Return to Shaftesbury Avenue and turn left to Great Windmill Street. Here is the **Red Lion** (13) at number 20, looking more like a Victorian library than a public drinking house. Karl Marx came here while living in nearby Dean Street and writing *Das Kapital*. Piccadilly Circus underground station is a little further along Shaftesbury Avenue.

12
From Newgate to Billingsgate

During the second century AD the Romans enclosed the city of London with a wall that stretched from the Tower of London in the south-east round through Aldgate and Cripplegate to Newgate and Ludgate, a distance of over 3 miles (4.8 km). One of the most important gates in those times was Newgate which, despite its name, was one of the earliest gates built by the Romans.

On the corner of Newgate Street and Giltspur Street is the **Viaduct Tavern** (1), which dates from 1869. Queen Victoria opened Holborn Viaduct on the same day in 1869 that she declared open Blackfriars Bridge. The tavern has a grand Victorian interior, with a beaten metal ceiling, and a manager's office that would serve well as a pulpit in a church. In the cellars are the remains of some of the cells of Newgate Prison, which was finally demolished in 1902.

Opposite the Central Criminal Courts, commonly called the Old Bailey (they stood in the *ballium*, or open space outside the city wall), is the **Magpie and Stump** (2). This public house is now part of an office building but the site has a history almost as long as that

(Left) The Magpie and Stump, Newgate.

(Right) The Baynard Castle, Queen Victoria Street.

75

of the Old Bailey. In *Tavern Anecdotes* by 'One of the Old School', published in the nineteenth century, there appears: 'Magpie and Stump — This bird sometimes rests on a stump so that association is not improper, although unmeaning. A house so named, in Newgate Street, serves good liquors, and as a booking office for errand-carts.' The Magpie and Stump was its original name, but it changed to the King of Denmark, doubtless because the husband of Queen Anne was Prince George of Denmark and many of the courtiers were Danish; at this time several streets changed their titles, too. In the 1930s it reverted to its original title, the Magpie and Stump. Until public hangings were finally abolished in 1868 the house was a favourite position for wealthy City merchants and others to watch the proceedings from the upper windows. The amount charged for breakfast and a window with a view varied from £10 to £50. The popularity of such spectacles was enormous: on one occasion forty

The Cockpit, St Andrew's Hill.

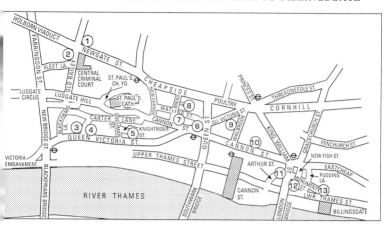

WALK 12: FROM NEWGATE TO BILLINGSGATE

1. The Viaduct Tavern
2. The Magpie and Stump
3. The Cockpit
4. The Baynard Castle
5. The Horn
6. Ye Olde Watling
7. The Pavilion End
8. Williamson's
9. Deacon's
10. The Cannon
11. The Bull Bear Broker
12. The Canterbury Arms
13. The Walrus and the Carpenter

thousand people came to watch. On that day twelve people were killed in the panic caused by a pie-man stumbling among the crowd. The landlord of the Magpie fared well that day for, after the crowds had departed, he collected several cartloads of shoes, coats, petticoats and hats from the ground surrounding the execution site. The customers who frequent the public house today include lawyers, detectives, jurors and others appearing at the Old Bailey opposite.

On the north side of the Old Bailey is a blue plaque stating that Newgate stood on the site until its demolition in the eighteenth century.

Walk along Newgate Street and turn right to St Paul's Cathedral. Opposite the cathedral is Deans Court, with the former Deanery on the right-hand side, and at the end you will find Carter Lane, still medieval in character. Turn right. Shortly after the old choir school on the left-hand side of the road, you come to St Andrew's Hill. Walk down the hill and on the left you will find the church of St Andrew by the Wardrobe and opposite it the **Cockpit** (3). It dates from the sixteenth century and would certainly have been familiar to William Shakespeare, who bought a house nearby in order to be close to the Blackfriars Theatre, which was the winter home of the players who performed during the summer at the Globe Theatre on Southwark's Bankside. They used the buildings of the former Blackfriars monastery, abandoned after the Dissolution of the Monasteries Act of 1539. It is not difficult to imagine the crowing and screeching of the cocks in the fights to the death that took place here. Cock fighting was banned in Britain in 1849, and shortly afterwards this house was renamed the Three Castles after the three buildings of nearby Baynard's Castle. However, a few years ago, it reverted to its original title and today the decor of the house features pictures of the old fighting cocks, and the bar has been arranged so as to recreate the pit and the gallery of the old cockpit of former times.

It is only a very short walk down the hill to the **Baynard Castle** (4) on the corner of Queen Victoria Street. Here the theme is medieval and revives the memory of the Norman fortress erected here during the time of William the Conqueror. According to Stow the first castle was built by a nobleman named Baynard who came to England with William. It was destroyed by King John in 1212 but rebuilt by Robert Fitzwalter later in the same century. When the Dominican (Black) Friars were granted land in the City in 1278 the castle was moved to a site opposite where the public house now stands and there it remained until the Great Fire of 1666, when it was severely damaged. Parts of the castle were turned into houses, but in the nineteenth century all traces were removed. There is a fine model of the castle in the Museum of London on London Wall. The museum houses other mementoes of past inns and taverns of London.

Turning up Queen Victoria Street, part of a nineteenth-century road improvement scheme, you pass the former British and Foreign Bible Society's headquarters and Faraday House, which, when built in 1932, was called a disgrace because its nine storeys would hide St Paul's Cathedral from view. The walker now comes to Godliman Street, at the side of the College of Arms, founded in the fifteenth century to grant coats of arms to appropriate people in England. Behind the College is Knightrider Street, once described as the longest in the City, when it led from the Tower of London to the King's Wardrobe by Baynard's Castle. At the far end is the **Horn** (5), a building founded in the late eighteenth century and handsomely rebuilt in recent years. The house is mentioned in early records as being the 'Horn Coffee House in Doctor's Commons', at a time when softer drinks were dispensed. Charles Dickens in *Pickwick Papers* has Mr Pickwick send his friends to the tavern to fetch a bottle of wine for his supper; today a marble bust of Dickens

The Horn, Knightrider Street.

dominates the bar. In company with some other public houses in the City it does not keep normal opening hours, closing at 9.30 pm, and having only a five-day licence.

From outside the Horn, St Paul's can be seen once more and after returning to its south side, past the City of London Information Centre, Cannon Street is reached. Walk down the street and Mansion House underground station is on the right-hand side. Opposite it is Bow Lane. Go up the lane and shortly Watling Street crosses over. On the corner is **Ye Olde Watling** (6), whose sign proclaims 'Rebuilt 1666'. Photographs taken early in the twentieth century show the house as a restaurant, and this is in keeping with its original licence, which clearly says that a meal must be ordered before the drinks.

A short walk along Watling Street is the **Pavilion End** (7) in a rebuilt nineteenth-century building, with sport showing every day on satellite television. Here the sports fan can drink while watching his favourite game.

For one of the most hidden taverns of the City the walker must continue up Bow Lane: on the left-hand side is the entrance to Groveland Court and **Williamson's** (8). It stands in a cul-de-sac alley, as it has done for two hundred years, secluded from the hustle and bustle of life in the City. In the eighteenth century a certain Mr Williamson turned the house on the site into an inn or tavern. Sir John Falstaff had owned a previous house on the site. The tavern

79

Ye Olde Watling, Watling Street.

had a large lounge that was used as a banqueting hall, and many people think that this was the original Mansion House, official residence of the Lord Mayor of London during his term of office. However, there is insufficient evidence to satisfy modern historians of this, but it is recorded that in the late seventeenth century the Lord Mayor did entertain the king and queen, William III and Mary, here on one occasion. They brought the Lord Mayor a gift, a fine pair of wrought iron gates. After these had been presented they were taken outside, but the queen promptly ordered their return to the hall. Today they can still be seen, outside, at the end of the alley. One of the pub's rooms is called the Mansion House Lounge, and there is also a stone declared to be in the centre of the City, though how this is measured is not stated. There is also a fireplace made from some Roman tiles that were found on the site during rebuilding after bomb damage in the Second World War.

After visiting Williamson's, the magnificent church of St Mary le Bow can be seen at the end of Bow Lane. This end of the lane leads directly into Cheapside, which in medieval days was three times its present width and was the main shopping centre of the City. At the end of the lane turn right into Cheapside and after passing King Street, which leads to the Guildhall, and Ironmonger Lane, with the Mercers' Company Hall, Old Jewry is on the left-hand side of the road just beyond where Cheapside becomes Poultry.

At the Bank intersection, one of the dominant buildings is the Mansion House, built in 1752 to the designs of George Dance the Elder at a cost of over £70,000. Sir Crisp Gascoigne was the first Lord Mayor to use it, in 1753. Beside it is the street called Walbrook after the river that flows underground beneath it today. On the right-hand side is **Deacon's** (9), which has acquired a reputation over the years of catering for younger people, and where on occasions girls outnumber boys. It is built into Bucklersbury House. During excavations for the foundations of the building the Mithraic temple of Roman London was found. The temple has now been rebuilt on the other side of the block in front of Temple Court, the offices of the Legal and General Insurance Company.

Continue down Walbrook to Cannon Street and turn left along it to the **Cannon** (10). Although the sign shows a cannon, the street name was originally Candlewick Street, home of candle makers in the middle ages. The pub is much frequented by bankers, brokers and other City folk.

Continue along Cannon Street to King William Street, where turn right. On the corner of Arthur Street is the **Bull Bear Broker** (11). Over the doorway is a modern-style inn-sign that shows the ups and downs of the Stock Market, by courtesy of Reuters News. If the Market is up on the previous day's rating a bear shows, if it is down the bull. The Market's performance is assessed every quarter of an hour.

The tall column visible from the front of the Bull Bear Broker is the Monument, designed by Sir Christopher Wren to commemorate the Great Fire of London. It stands 202 feet (62 metres) high, the distance from its base to the spot in Pudding Lane where the fire started in the king's baker's shop. The column stands on the site of one of the first churches to be destroyed in the fire, St Margaret's, New Fish Street, in whose parish is also to be found the **Canterbury Arms** (12). It takes its name from the Canterbury pilgrims who started their pilgrimage to the shrine of St Thomas Becket from the chapel on old London Bridge which was also dedicated to the saint, who was born in London's Cheapside. There has been a tavern on this site since at least the fourteenth century, although the present building dates from the twentieth. Among the unusual items to be found here are the Beadle's tricorn hat and his truncheon.

Continue down to Lower Thames Street and the site of Billingsgate. This was never a fortified entrance into the city but a dock or hithe — an inlet into the riverbank where goods could be safely unloaded from ships. Tradition has it that its original owner and builder was a merchant by the name of Belling or Billing. The story says that on his death he was cremated and his ashes were placed in an urn, which was then put on top of the gate that divided the river from the dock. Recent excavation revealed the medieval dock and, although the site has been filled in again for redevelopment, a full record has been made of the excavation.

Billingsgate Fish Market was here until it was moved downstream to the Isle of Dogs, Poplar Dock, in 1981. The market had existed here since being granted its royal charter in 1699 and stood near the site of the original Billingsgate dock. Like the workers at other London markets, Billingsgate's workers had local inns and taverns where they could refresh themselves when other drinkers were barred by the licensing laws.

Our last call is reached by turning left along Lower Thames Street to Lovat Lane, at the junction with Monument Street. Lord Lovat was the last man to be publicly beheaded on Tower Hill, and at the river end of the lane named after him stands the **Walrus and the Carpenter** (13). It replaces the Cock tavern where the fish porters of Billingsgate could obtain a drink 'out of hours' by virtue of their calling.

13
Clerkenwell —
a drink by the Clerks' Well

The earliest mention of Clerks' Well is in the twelfth-century description of London by Fitzstephen, the biographer of St Thomas Becket. He records: 'amongst which Holy Wells, Clerkenwell … are most noted and most frequently visited by the scholars from the schools as by the youths of the City…'. Throughout the middle ages the Worshipful Company of Parish Clerks regularly performed mystery plays on the banks of the Fleet River for the 'spiritual education of the people'. Today it may stretch the imagination to think of the populace coming here for as long as three days, as they did in 1390 when the king and his court attended *The Passion of Our Lord* and *The Creation* here. They doubtless drank the waters of the well during the intermissions. Nowadays stronger liquids are served in the many interesting inns in the area.

A short distance away from Farringdon station, the terminus of London's first underground railway, is the **Castle** (1). George IV is said to have attended a cockfight nearby in the early nineteenth century. Apparently he ran out of money, so, having a sure winner in the next round, he went to the Castle and persuaded the landlord to loan him £5, using his father's watch as a security. The king won the bet and returned the money to the landlord, who, it is claimed, had not recognised him. The landlord was offered a knighthood, which he refused, but he did accept the right to act as a pawnbroker. The three balls, the pawnbrokers' sign, hang outside the house, but whether you can hock anything here today is not clear. The hanging sign shows the Tower of London, with an inn at the entrance displaying the pawnbrokers' sign. A painting of George IV and his visit hangs on the wall of the bar.

The Castle, Cowcross Street: the pawnbrokers' sign.

Cross over the road to the **Three Compasses** (2), first established on this site in 1723. The modern building comprises a bar on the ground floor and an excellent restaurant on the first floor, from whose window one can watch the numerous people who use the street to get to and from Smithfield Market. The sign shows three compasses, an instrument used by three of the ancient livery companies of the City, the Carpenters, the Stone Masons and the Shipwrights.

On leaving the public house turn right and follow Cowcross Street until the **Hope** (3) is reached. The name is a corruption of one of the earliest inn signs, the Hoops and Grapes, derived from the hoops of the barrels of beer in the cellars of the house. The tavern will delight the artistically minded, because of the superbly etched glass panels, the mirrors, and the architectural detail of this Victorian building. Both inside and outside there is much on offer — and the beer is good too!

Across the roadway from the Hope is St John Street. Keep to its left-hand side and soon the **White Bear** (4) is reached. This is the last of some fifteen drinking houses that existed here a hundred years ago, at a time when distances to and from London were still being measured from Hicks House, which stood on the opposite side of the roadway. Hicks House was a sessions house erected in the seventeenth century by Sir Baptist Hicks and was used for the trial of the regicides, who had convicted Charles I and condemned him to death. Sir Baptist's father was a silk mercer in Soper Lane near the White Bear in Cheapside. This inn always offers a warm welcome to guests.

Continue to walk along St John Street until reaching Passing Alley. Turn left along this and carry on to St John's Lane. Here, to the right, can be seen the gateway to the precinct of the Knights Hospitallers of the Order of St John of Jerusalem. Walk under the archway and on the left is the **St John of Jerusalem** (5). This building commemorates two former drinking houses: the original tavern, which stood until 1760 on the corner of Jerusalem Passage, and the gatehouse, which itself was at one time used as an inn. To appreciate the part that they have played in the past here one should examine the various illustrations on the wall of the bar — after having first sampled one of the various lagers on sale.

Care should be taken in crossing Clerkenwell Road just to the left of the house on leaving. The road divided St John's Square in two, one part containing the public house and the other the remains of the priory church. On the far side of the square is Jerusalem Passage, at the end of which is Aylesbury Street. Turn right and walk along to Woodbridge Street, at the other end of which is the **Sekforde Arms** (6). After his retirement in the sixteenth century Thomas Sekforde,

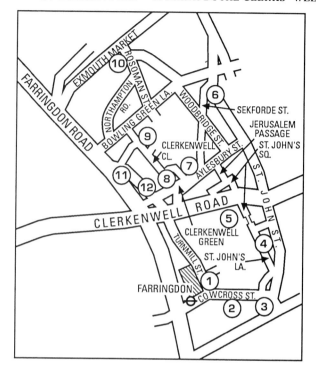

WALK 13: CLERKENWELL — A DRINK BY THE CLERKS' WELL

1. *The Castle*
2. *The Three Compasses*
3. *The Hope*
4. *The White Bear*
5. *The St John of Jerusalem*
6. *The Sekforde Arms*
7. *The Crown Tavern*
8. *The Kings of Clerkenwell*
9. *The Horseshoe*
10. *The London Spa*
11. *The Betsy Trotwood*
12. *The City Pride*

or Seckford, settled in a house nearby. He was the patron of Christopher Saxton, the English cartographer who made and recorded the earliest topographical survey of Britain. The arms on the signboard are those of Thomas Sekforde, whose family spanned over three hundred years. This inn is a good village-type family tavern.

By walking down Sekforde Street, Clerkenwell Green and the **Crown Tavern** (7) are reached. Built on the site of a medieval hostelry, the present building dates from the nineteenth century. The house has snob-screens, which enable the observer to see through into the next bar without being seen doing so. On the walls are a collection of playbills from the Apollo Company, who used to perform in the upper room. The time is told by a clock said to have come from Rye House in Hertfordshire. The house was the scene of the Rye House Plot in 1683, an alleged conspiracy of Whigs to kill Charles II on his way back from the Newmarket races; the plot was unsuccessful. The house next to the tavern, now demolished, was used by Oliver Cromwell in the earlier part of the seventeenth century. Note the doorway marked GIN, and the side window of another etched with the words COFFEE HOUSE.

A few yards away in Clerkenwell Close is the **Kings of Clerkenwell** (8), which served as the hostelry for the nearby Benedictine nunnery before the Dissolution of the Monasteries in 1539. Doubtless originally the name was the Three Kings, a reference to the Magi who visited Christ at Bethlehem. The present signboard shows other kings: Elvis Presley (King of Rock), Henry VII (King of England) and King Kong! On the other side are three conventional kings' crowns. Both signs are three-dimensional but should not distract the visitor from entering. It was not unusual in former times for inns and taverns to be used for the holding of inquests and trials. One of the more infamous trials that took place here was that in 1834 of Steinberg, who was accused of murdering his common-law wife and her children.

Clerkenwell Close twists and turns until it reaches the **Horseshoe** (9), standing on the corner and almost overwhelmed by the surrounding buildings. According to tradition a tunnel leads from the house to the nearby house of correction and was used by the hangman when going about his macabre duty. The prison has long since disappeared and the site is now occupied by the Hugh Myddelton Schools. It was the abortive attempt by Michael Barrett in 1867 to rescue fellow members of the Fenian Party from the prison that led to his being hanged outside the Newgate Prison in 1868. His was the last public hanging in England. In the crowd outside the prison was Charles Dickens, protesting against public hanging, but not apparently against the death sentence.

After visiting the pub follow the line of the roadway around and cross over Bowling Green Lane into Northampton Road, at the end of which are Rosoman Street and the **London Spa** (10). The present building marks the site of an old inn called the Fountain. A chalybeate spring (containing iron) was first discovered here in 1206 and by the eighteenth century had become a famous health and entertainment centre. The remains of these spa buildings are to be found in the cellar of the present house. During the nineteenth century the house was converted into a gin palace and attracted a different type of customer. This in turn attracted ladies of loose morals and it became a house of ill-repute. Today all that is history and its fittings and furnishings reflect the 'good old days'.

From the London Spa walk along the Exmouth Market to Farringdon Road. Here turn left and walk down the road to the **Betsey Trotwood** (11), which stands on the corner at the junction of Farringdon Road and Farringdon Lane. Miss Betsy Trotwood was the great-aunt of David Copperfield in Dickens's novel and later became his guardian. She lived in a cottage on the way to Highgate and may well have passed by here on her way home. This is another pleasant corner pub that warrants a visit or two to take in the convivial atmosphere. On the rear wall overlooking the railway lines of the Underground is a mural depicting local industry in the nineteenth century.

From here it is a short walk down Farringdon Lane to the **City Pride** (12), whose signboard proudly displays the City of London arms, the cross of St George of England and the sword of St Paul, which are supported by the two griffins of Fuller's Brewery, the landlords. It feels as if one is visiting somebody's private house, so cunningly has the interior been designed. The downstairs bar came from the Star and Garter near Kew Bridge. There are also a number of tradesmen's signboards to interest the visitor during a stay here. Nearby is the Clerks' Well, admission to which can be obtained from the Finsbury Public Library in Skinner Street.

Go back to Farringdon Road and turn left to return to Farringdon station.

The Crown Tavern, Clerkenwell. The reassuring motto over the door reads: 'Be not forgetful to entertain strangers — for thereby some have entertained angels.'

The Duke of York, Harrowby Street.

14
Marylebone —
knights, doctors and criminals

The former Borough of St Marylebone grew out of one of the 'lost villages' of London, with housing developments in the seventeenth and eighteenth centuries joining the cities of London and Westminster together. Maps of these times show houses being built along the road to Oxford, and in the nineteenth century John Nash laid out Regent Street and Portland Place. In addition to the streets, squares were laid out in the fashion of the times. Wealthy and noble families moved in and with them came hordes of servants. In the north of the former borough is St John's Wood, where the land was once owned by the Knights of the Order of St John of Jerusalem. At the time of the Dissolution of the Monasteries in the sixteenth century these estates were confiscated and divided up into two parcels of land. One, owned by John Lyon, the founder of Harrow School, was later bequeathed to the school. Charles II gave the larger estate to the third Lord Wotton. Later this estate was sold to Henry Eyre, a merchant of the City of London.

Just behind the Marks and Spencer store in Oxford Street (not far from Marble Arch station) can be found Portman Mews South and the **Three Tuns** (1) public house. The present building was built early in the nineteenth century and replaced an earlier one. It is one of the inns that offered refreshment to felons being taken to Tyburn for execution. When visiting the house in the winter, it is a joy to sit by the coal fire to eat and drink. There is a small collection of mounted butterflies in a display unit in the bar. The signboard shows three barrel (tun) ends with a frothing pewter tankard in front.

Leading out of Portman Square in the north-west corner is Upper Berkeley Street, where at number 51 is the **Masons' Arms** (2). It is a popular pub, but like the previous one it has grim reminders of the past. The cellars here were used in former times to deposit criminals in overnight, possibly when the Tyburn Tree was becoming overcrowded with bodies. Needless to say, it is said that the cellars are haunted by a ghost or two from those gruesome days. The tunnel through which they walked to their executions was sealed up some years ago.

Off the Edgware Road is Harrowby Street, where one can find the **Duke of York** (3), with its tables and chairs, potted plants and window-boxes outside in fine weather. Inside there is a collection of ceramic figures of famous personalities, including representatives of the world of sport. The clientele is mainly made up of sportsmen, amateur and professional, as well as their fans.

The next street up is Crawford Place, which leads into Crawford Street. Here on the corner of Homer Street is the **Quintin Hogg** (4), formerly the Olive Branch. The house was officially opened by Lord Hailsham of St Marylebone, who as Quintin Hogg represented the borough in the House of Commons from 1963 to 1970 and later served as Lord Chancellor. He unveiled a plaque on the outside wall and pulled the first pint in the newly refurbished house. The decorative theme, appropriately, is a legal one and includes a large mirror depicting a policeman and a judge dominating the view from behind the bar.

Also in Crawford Street, on the corner of Wyndham Place, is the **Duke of Wellington** (5), described as a 'small and friendly place'. The frontage is designed in the style of an antique shop. In the windows is a large collection of Wellingtoniana, while from a blocked side window the Duke himself looks down on the passing crowds with a tankard in his hand.

The Quintin Hogg, Homer Street.

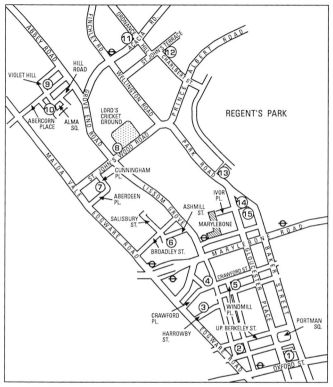

WALK 14: MARYLEBONE— KNIGHTS, DOCTORS AND CRIMINALS
1. The Three Tuns
2. The Masons' Arms
3. The Duke of York
4. The Quintin Hogg
5. The Duke of Wellington
6. The Marquis of Anglesea
7. Crocker's
8. The Lord's Tavern
9. The Abbey Tavern
10. The Heroes of Alma
11. The Ordnance Arms
12. The Star
13. The Windsor Castle
14. The Gloucester
15. The Volunteer

Beyond the Marylebone Road, which was London's first bypass, built in the eighteenth century, is Lisson Grove, out of which runs Ashmill Street. Here is the **Marquis of Anglesea** (6), a good Victorian house with an atmosphere to match its age. The gaslights are augmented by electric ones delicately shaded so as not to spoil the old-world atmosphere. Nearby in Lisson Street there is a toddlers'

The Duke of Wellington. (Above) The sign. (Below) The display of Wellingtoniana in the window.

play area as well as a place for the foot-weary to sit and rest.

Opposite the pub is Salisbury Street, which leads to Broadley Street. Turn left and walk along it back to the Edgware Road. Turn right. Walk along to Aberdeen Place. Here is **Crocker's** (7), which earned the nickname of 'Crocker's Folly'. Crocker was the man who had this house built, in late Victorian classical style, as a station hotel. However, he had misjudged where Marylebone railway station was going to be built. In desperation he threw himself from the roof. He is said to haunt the premises from time to time, when he plays with anything mechanical that he can lay his hands on.

It is a pleasant walk through Cunningham Place, named after a vicar of Harrow, the Reverend John William Cunningham, and part of the Lyon estate. At the end of the road turn right and walk along St John's Wood Road to the **Lord's Tavern** (8), built in 1966 to replace an earlier one. Thomas Lord founded the Marylebone Cricket Club in 1787 and laid out his first cricket ground in Dorset Square. In 1809 he moved to North Bank, St John's Wood, after he learned that his rent was going to rise to what was in his opinion an unacceptable level. With the construction of the Regent's Canal in 1814 he moved to the present site, building the first Lord's Tavern. All early cricket grounds had attached to them an inn or tavern, where the two teams could retire at the end of the day's play.

Return towards the Edgware Road and turn right along Maida Vale to reach Abercorn Place, off which is Violet Hill, which is the boundary between the two estates, the Harrow School (Lyon) and the Eyre. The road is all that is left of a medieval lane that once linked Lisson village to Kilburn Priory. Here is the **Abbey Tavern** (9). It once had archery grounds attached to it, but the present nineteenth-century building contains a fine collection of Spy cartoons, as well as providing a good pint or two for the thirsty.

Opposite Violet Hill is Nugent Terrace, which leads to Alma Square and the **Heroes of Alma** (10). Its earliest extant title deed, dated 24th December 1872, includes a clause requiring the owner 'to conduct the business of the said Public House, Inn or Tavern under the name of and constantly keep up the effigy or sign of the "Heroes of Alma"'. In Alma Square you will look in vain for an open square because the grass area lies at the backs of the houses of the square, which was laid out in 1862. The Battle of Alma was fought during the Crimean War on 20th September 1854, when the combined armies of Britain, France and Turkey, under the joint command of General Lord Raglan and General St Arnaud, routed the Russian army. The house stands in a little cul-de-sac in one corner of the square.

From Alma Square walk north-east along Hill Road, turn right in Abbey Road, then left in Grove End Road to cross over Finchley

Road/Wellington Road by the side of St John's Wood underground station and walk along Acacia Road to Ordnance Hill and the **Ordnance Arms** (11). Here, in a quiet backwater, it is possible to have a drink inside or at the tables in front of the house. The saloon was once described as being 'the smallest, well-worn and well-mannered room that is at the same time discreetly intimate'. The site in former times was occupied by one of the many farms of the Knights Templars' estate.

At the foot of Ordnance Hill is St John's Wood Terrace. Turn left and across the roadway is the **Star** (12), on the corner of Charlbert Street. As the area developed in the 1830s so did the need for more drinking establishments, and so the Star was built. While the decor has been described as being 'of a real antique flavour', the welcome is certainly modern.

Charlbert Street leads down to Prince Albert Road and Regent's Park. A pleasant walk though the park, when it is open, makes a change from the stone pavements, but leave the park to turn along Kent Passage and follow it to Park Road. Turn left. Shortly will be seen the **Windsor Castle** (13), with its signboard displaying the castle. The building is classical in design with a bow front and crenellations at roof level. Note the fine wrought-iron railing outside the first-floor windows. The house stands at the end of a terrace of shops with housing above.

On the corner of Gloucester Place and Ivor Place (shown on nineteenth-century maps as Upper Park Place, but changed to Ivor Place in 1934 by the then London County Council for no apparent or logical reason) stands the **Gloucester** (14), a late Victorian house in the classical style with a contemporary interior design enhanced by the delicate use of 'electric gas-lighting'. Outside seating is provided in the form of picnic tables and chairs, where one can sit and watch the world pass by.

At the point where Baker Street meets Park Road is the **Volunteer** (15), now fully restored to being a public house once more, having been converted for a while into a café. The house dates from 1794 and replaces a farmhouse that stood on the site in the seventeenth century. It was during this time that the estate was owned by the Nevill family, one of whom fought at the battle of Naseby in June 1645. Nine years later the entire family perished in a fire that destroyed the farmhouse. One of the family, Rupert Nevill, is said to haunt the cellar of the house. He has been seen by a recent owner 'wearing a surcoat, breeches and stockings' dating from the seventeenth century. Lights have been known to be inexplicably turned on and off, and footsteps have been heard when the bar was shut up for the night. There are bus stops nearby in Baker Street, and Baker Street underground station is also close at hand.